Become an author faster
and transform your expertise
into business gold

LUCY McCARRAHER

Re^think

First published in Great Britain in 2025
by Rethink Press (www.rethinkpress.com)

© Copyright Lucy McCarraher

All rights reserved. No part of this publication may be reproduced, stored in or introduced into a retrieval system, or transmitted, in any form, or by any means (electronic, mechanical, photocopying, recording or otherwise) without the prior written permission of the publisher.

The right of Lucy McCarraher to be identified as the author of this work has been asserted by her in accordance with the Copyright, Designs and Patents Act 1988.

This book is sold subject to the condition that it shall not, by way of trade or otherwise, be lent, resold, hired out, or otherwise circulated without the publisher's prior consent in any form of binding or cover other than that in which it is published and without a similar condition including this condition being imposed on the subsequent purchaser.

Cover image © Shutterstock | Cesare Andrea Ferrari

Illustrations by Andrew Priestley

CONTENTS

Foreword		1
Introduction		7
1	The Goldmine	13
	The Storytellers	14
	Your Goldmine	22
	The Golden Keys	30
	Book Magic	39
2	Prospecting	43
	Ore, Nuggets and Dust	44
	3Ps of Positioning	49
	Title and Subtitle	56
3	Mining	65
	The Gold in Your IP	66
	The Five-step Book Introduction	69

	The Magic Book Plan	76
	Your Book Blueprint	83
4	**Extracting**	**87**
	Separating Gold from Ore	88
	Your AUTHOR Mindset	89
	Research	93
	Your Author Voice	97
	The WRITER Process	101
	Writing Your First Draft	104
	The Emotional Journey	113
5	**Refining**	**117**
	Fire and Acid	118
	Review	119
	Improve	122
	Test	125
	Edit	130
	Repeat	132
	The Foreword	133
6	**The Golden Key**	**137**
	Creating Gold Bars	138
	Traditional Publishing	139
	DIY/Self-publishing	147

Hybrid Publishing	151
Promote Your Book to Build Your Business	164
Conclusion: Book Magic	**171**
Bibliography	**179**
Acknowledgements	**183**
The Author	**185**

FOREWORD

Think back over the last five years and ask yourself, 'Have I been of value to others?'

Have you done work with people that got great results? Have you delivered outcomes people were happy to pay you for? Have you solved painful problems or removed nagging frustrations? Have you told stories that others engaged with? Have you shared insights that lit people up? Have you sparked big ideas or inspired creativity through conversations?

If you have, you have a goldmine of intellectual property that should be shared with more people in a book.

The book that changes your life the most is not one that you read; it's one that you write. No amount of articles, blogs, podcasts or books that you consume will come close to the impact of what you produce. Writing and publishing a book is a powerful step in your career or business.

For centuries, a book was an elite-level format, reserved for only a chosen few. To write a book you needed a publisher to fund it and coordinate distribution. Traditional publishers were the gatekeepers to getting books produced and distributed through bookshops – individual authors couldn't access these services themselves.

Today, things are different. Global distribution is easy, thanks to the likes of Amazon and Audible. A book can be published on the Kindle Store on a Monday morning and later that afternoon find itself being read in Brisbane, Bogota, Botswana and Birmingham. Billions of dollars have been invested into innovations that have made book publishing accessible to anyone.

The next big barrier to come down is the writing process. For many years, professional writers have had expensive teams of literary professionals helping them brainstorm, structure, write, edit and improve their work. Today, artificial intelligence can provide that support at a fraction of the cost. Any author can make use of a powerful AI tool that does the work of a coaching, writing and editing team – something that only the most famous authors of the past would have enjoyed.

You are reading this book at a magical time in history when the writing process has become highly supported by AI, the publishing process has never been more accessible and the global distribution of books has never been more extensive.

Now it's your turn to write a life-changing book. A book that shares your knowledge with the world and turns your readers into your next clients.

In 2010, my first book, *Become a Key Person of Influence*, was published. Since then, I've had countless opportunities come from it. It's helped me to meet amazing people, get featured in the media, speak on big stages and scale a business globally.

I've witnessed first-hand what a vital tool a published book is for many other business owners. Being the author of a good book is one of the best ways I know to effortlessly demonstrate your value, attract more interest, increase your influence and raise your income.

I've seen Dominic Colenso write *Impact* and build a wildly successful speaker-training business off the back of it. I've seen Jeroen Van De Waal publish *Together We Can Turn Tides* and spark both an ocean conservation movement and a fast-growth business.

Donna O'Toole wrote *Win*, and it has catapulted her awards agency to new heights.

A book is a powerful asset for attracting clients. Your book goes out into the world and networks with people on your behalf, shares key ideas with them and, in many cases, facilitates a direct sales enquiry. A book tells people about the goldmine of wisdom you possess and brings interested parties into your business.

A book also creates credibility and tells the world that its creator is an authority in their field. It's no coincidence that the word 'authority' contains the word 'author'.

Having worked with thousands of entrepreneurs, professionals and leaders across fifty industries, in over a dozen countries, we've found that over a third of our clients who publish a book double their income in under two years. The process of writing (especially with the support of AI) makes you smarter. It sharpens communication skills, develops a thought leadership stance and clarifies thinking around themes and trends on a topic.

In a recent report, *A Comprehensive Study of Business Book ROI*, it was revealed that authors who had a revenue strategy linked to their book made over $100,000 in revenue, on average, within six months of launching their book. They earned this money by raising awareness of their topic, delivering value to others and gaining exciting opportunities in media and on stage.

For all of these reasons, you are wise to consider writing a book – and you've come to the right place for support in doing it well.

Lucy McCarraher has been the Publish Mentor for Dent and the Key Person of Influence programme since 2013. Lucy has mentored hundreds, if not thousands, of entrepreneurs through her inspired system of planning and writing business books, and then published them through Rethink Press.

I work with Lucy, alongside Joe Gregory, to produce and publish my books: they take my rough draft manuscript and turn it into a high-quality publication. With decades of experience, they know all the tweaks and refinements that are needed to create a successful book. In the UK business book charts, at any given time you'll see a number of their titles in the top ten bestsellers – because they know what works.

Lucy is also the guiding force behind Book Magic AI. Her insights on writing and publishing form the backbone of one of the most powerful AI tools for authors.

While the barriers to entry for writing and publishing a book are now lower than ever, the barriers to excellence have never been higher. There are more books being published, people can share their review with the world in an instant, and there has never been more competition for your market's time and attention.

In a global marketplace powered by digital platforms, published content is the key to attracting highly valuable opportunities from far and wide, and a book is the supreme published format. There's no doubt, if you are embarking on the journey of writing a book, you can look forward to many rewards.

If you intend to write a book that you can be proud of, one that will establish your authority and get your message out to your audience in a big way, I urge you to read *Book Magic* – the latest and most refined methodology for planning and writing an excellent business book from the pre-eminent expert in the field.

Your book needs to be a great book. Lucy and *Book Magic* will make sure it is.

Daniel Priestley

Bestselling author, entrepreneur and founder of Dent Global

INTRODUCTION

As an expert or entrepreneur, coach or consultant, speaker or leader, you are standing on a goldmine of knowledge and experience. Hidden underground is the precious substance that shines out in your work with clients; the mighty foundation you've built your business on; the deep source of energy that powers your mission and vision. However, as long as it remains buried in that mine, only revealed to the few who pay for a guided tour, it isn't bringing either you or your market the full value of its wealth.

The veins of golden ore you are guarding in your mine include the years of experience you have from working in your business or area of expertise, the knowledge you've absorbed from being a substantial contributor to your industry, along with the historical perspective you've gained and the future you envision for it. The nuggets you have beneath your feet include the innovative processes you've developed for working with your clients and the outcomes you've produced for them. The genius you've applied to building your business to its current success is pure gold dust.

From your vantage point atop this goldmine, I think you know it's time. Time to extract the treasure you are sitting on, shape and polish it into a dazzling asset and offer it to the wider world.

Time to transition from well-thought-of expert to thought-leading author.

Perhaps what's stopped you getting on with this transition is that you don't know how to get started on that journey. This is where I come in.

Like you, I'm an expert in my field, a successful entrepreneur and founder of businesses. Like you, I've developed processes and tools to take my clients from concept to results when they work with me, and found innovative repeatable methods to solve seemingly intractable problems. However, unlike you, my area of expertise is books – writing, publishing and mentoring others through the process of creating beautifully crafted volumes that amplify their voices in crowded markets, magnetise their ideal clients and transform their businesses in ways they didn't think possible.

INTRODUCTION

I am the UK's most experienced business book mentor, having guided well over a thousand expert authors through the process of writing and publishing their book. In 2011, with Joe Gregory I founded Rethink Press, now the biggest hybrid publisher of business books in the UK; I founded and am CEO of Book Magic AI, the unique AI-supported book-writing app; and I've written fourteen books (including this one) myself. You could say that I've spent the last fifteen years transforming industry experts into influential authors. I've mined my own models for planning and writing books, and helped others to hone their precious knowledge into glittering trophies. I'm here to sprinkle my gold dust around the voyage of discovery that writing your book is going to be. My goal for you is not just to write a book, but to craft your legacy and create a powerful tool that unlocks your shining future.

If I had a pound for every entrepreneur, coach or consultant who has told me they're going to write their book 'this year' and didn't, and hasn't ever become a published author, I wouldn't need a goldmine. However, if so many experts want to write their book and don't actually do it, what's going on?

In my experience there are a few key challenges that stop someone getting a good and valuable book written and published, and the first is very simple: they don't know where to start. Like you, they are the expert in their field, but when it comes to a substantial new project like writing a book, they become the novice. Other people make a start, but don't realise that positioning and detailed planning have to come before writing, and dive straight in. Within a few chapters they get overwhelmed by what feels like a huge amorphous task, stop writing and often never restart. Recently, I spoke to an entrepreneur who had fourteen unfinished manuscripts on their PC!

Another big mistake is to believe that writing a book is a solo task. We carry a mental image of the creative writer, scratching away with their quill pen (or tapping away at their keyboard) in a lonely garret – but going it alone without support, expert help or accountability is another ingredient in the recipe for an unfinished book.

This book is me holding out my hand to you, ready to guide you through the glorious but challenging transition from expert to author.

In *Book Magic* you'll learn the steps to mining the precious metal of your knowledge and expertise. Gold mining is a four-step process: prospecting, mining, extracting and refining. I'll show you how to prospect for your perfect readers – your ideal clients, promoters and partners – and when we've located the sweet spot we'll go through the steps for mining the ore of your unique value proposition and leveraging it in your book. I'll show you how to extract the perfect structure out of your deep experience to provide maximum

INTRODUCTION

impact and reader engagement, and we'll work together on refining that value into polished and compelling written content. Like mining, the Book Magic process is as much science as art, based on years of research with a wide range of entrepreneur and expert authors, and now distilled into the gold standard of book-creation.

Working with me, you'll become confident in your writing abilities so you can stay motivated through your author journey. I know that mentoring an author through writing a book requires constancy, consistency and empathy. I am genuinely here for you – through this book and in the Book Magic AI app. After all, we're not just writing a book, we're positioning you at the forefront of your industry now and crafting your legacy into the future. Your book is the key that will open doors to new opportunities, from standing out as the authority in your field to stepping forward onto stages and other speaking engagements. This is not just about putting words on a page; it's about writing your glowing future.

We start your Book Magic journey by prospecting with the 3Ps of Position – a simple but effective tool that yields absolute clarity on your ideal reader and client (Person), identifies their fundamental challenges (Pain) and articulates the transformation your book will offer them (Promise). Moving on to the Planning phase, we'll dig down into the topics, stories and data you'll reveal for your readers and organise them into a detailed and compelling structure of chapters and parts. Then the deep mining starts with you writing your first draft – the first step in the WRITER Process. This acronym takes you through a chunked and closely defined set of steps for what can otherwise feel like a titanic task with no boundaries: Write (your first draft), Review and Improve (together make up your first self-edit), Test (your second draft with carefully chosen beta readers), Edit (for the last time, consolidating and incorporating the best feedback), and finally Repeat (any steps) until you have a final writer's manuscript to submit for professional editing and publishing.

This book will give you the overview and the detail I've accumulated over years – it's not just a book but the blueprint for your authorial success. To keep you on track and on the cutting edge, you'll see how Book Magic AI can be your powerful ally, enhancing your creativity and efficiency.

Now let's get to work on your book – your golden key to future success.

ONE
THE GOLDMINE

THE STORYTELLERS

From the dawn of time, when humans lived in tribes and passed on knowledge from generation to generation by word of mouth, tribal experts were the storytellers: the leaders who acquired and then passed on knowledge, experience, inspiring stories and cultural values.

Business books today tap into the most ancient practice of passing on vital information to improve lives. All experts and entrepreneurs that I've encountered have a compulsion to pass on their knowledge to the rest of the tribe.

Humans took a massive leap when they found ways of recording stories for posterity, not confined to singular events where one person spoke to others, but ways of passing on knowledge from one generation to the next. The earliest wall paintings were possibly the first kind of self-help guides. Those who were most skilled in painting or carving pictures, scenes of activity, were the leaders, the experts, the authorities. Until…

Pictures became pictograms and eventually alphabets that enabled our ancestors to express thoughts as written words. Words that strung together as sentences; sentences that combined into paragraphs; paragraphs that described facts and listed figures, developed ideas and concepts, created permanent cultures and civilisations.

Words became power – and embedding those words in stone or wood, on leather or papyrus meant they spoke across the constraints of time and place.

The ability to write was for leaders – the very few; the ability to read was for followers – but only selected groups. Even though the Chinese were printing with woodblocks in the ninth century, and the Koreans were using moveable metal type in the fourteenth century, the written word was precious, constrained and limited by the difficulties of reproduction – until…

In 1437, German goldsmith Johannes Gutenberg devised a printing press that incorporated a screw-type wine press to squeeze down evenly on the inked metal type. This simple innovation is what suddenly enabled the cheap mass-production of books on every imaginable topic: revolutionary ideas and priceless knowledge were placed in the hands of every literate European, whose numbers doubled every century. You could say that mass printing was the start of the Reading Revolution. Books could now change lives at scale.

The book became the iconic format of expertise: simple, accessible, flexible, portable and aesthetically pleasing – sometimes works of art in their own right. From that time, and still six centuries later, books hold the power and generate the magic of the ancient storytellers. Books spread ideas. Books inform, entertain and educate at scale.

Everyone (give or take) can read a book, or listen to an audiobook, so up until now it's been easy to be a reader – a follower – but much harder to become an author – a leader. Publishers used to be the gatekeepers to authors getting their books produced and distributed. Then Amazon, print-on-demand and self-publishing came along and removed most of the barriers to publishing.

But there is still a barrier to writing a *good* book – especially a good book that will build your business. Currently, reading is for everyone; the availability of books in all formats means we are all consumers of information through books – and the books you read can change your life.

But now we are at the cutting edge of the Author Revolution.

Book Magic AI, along with this book, is moving the dial from everyone being able to consume information to everyone being able to *create* information. Importantly, that doesn't mean handing over the content creation to ChatGPT or other large language models (LLM).

Most of the authors whose books we publish at Rethink Press worked with us in person to get their books written. The high-quality, in-person book coaching we offer can cost a substantial amount of money, and that can be the barrier to loads of excellent books getting stuck in their authors' heads. Now the Book Magic vision is to take the latest technology and tap into the ancient needs and desires to share experience, tell stories and pass on knowledge through the power of words. To enable all entrepreneurs to create a game-changing asset for their business. I hope that you'll take advantage of the brilliant software in the app that helps you put into practice all the steps and information that I'm going to take you through in this book.

Where has the Book Magic book-writing methodology come from and why is it so special and, indeed, unique?

The Book Magic book-writing programme has been built on a decade's worth of in-depth experience from coaching and mentoring experts and entrepreneurs who have gone through the process of writing a book to build their business. Thanks to the collaboration between Rethink Press and the Key Person of Influence programme, I personally have mentored around 2,000 authors through their writing process over the last ten years. Rethink Press – uniquely in the publishing industry – has built an extraordinary team of business book-writing coaches and ghostwriters who have worked one-to-one with hundreds of authors, using the same process.

All this experience has flowed into the Book Magic book and app, and you can access person-to-person support through the Book Magic live coaching team to back up the Book Magic AI coaches who guide you in the app.

Our three-step process is one of a kind. Among all the business book coaches and writing programmes out there – and there aren't many I don't know – ours is the only successful, repeatable framework with clear, proven models for positioning, planning and writing a book that demonstrably will build both the author's authority and their business.

As well as the Book Magic steps that have been honed over a decade of practical work with real-life authors, this book and the coaching app make use of cutting-edge learning theory. When I did my postgrad diploma in teaching adult literacy and creative writing, we were still using Fleming's (2001) now discredited VARK learning styles. Current research shows that there are only two key learning styles: expert and novice. In this context, experts are people who have developed extensive mental models in a specific field through years of experience. This allows them to assess challenges rapidly and respond fluently, efficiently and successfully. I am the expert in book writing, and so, consequently, is the Book Magic AI app. Novices, on the other hand, benefit from explicit instruction: seeing models, hearing explanations and practising small steps, which is exactly how I support you here, and the app supports you, the author, through learning to write a great book.

However, you are also the expert in your own field and, in that sense, far from a novice. While I'm here to give you tried-and-tested models and outlines for book writing, it's crucial that you remain in control of your own expertise – and if I or the AI coach or structure suggest something that doesn't feel right to you, you are the expert and should go with your own best intelligence. I never want to patronise or infantilise you, or any expert author, by telling you to write a book to a one-size-fits-all structure, or suggest that the AI knows better than you.

I also know that there are two fundamental types of mental processing: internal processors, who tend to think by writing; and external processors, who often think by speaking. Whether you're working in the Book Magic AI app, which provides both options, or in your own software, choose the easiest way for you to get the words out of your head and onto the page. Or do a bit of both. Don't make it an excuse for not getting your book written!

Perhaps my greatest learning over my decade of book mentoring is that the most important thing I can do for an author, the thing that will ensure they finish writing their book, is to be there for them all the way, to the bitter end, however short or long it takes. Therefore, I'm here for you in this book whatever stage you're at. I suggest that you read it all the way through first and then come back to the detail as you work through the different stages. There's an AI version of me in the Book Magic app, among other AI coaches, and if you're a paid subscriber you can join the Book Magic Community Facebook group, ask me questions there and log onto my regular live Zoom calls. Book Magic is not a finite programme where the coach has a timeline and then moves on to their next cohort, or a course that closes before you've finished writing. I'm here until you get it done.

Book Magic is based on ten years of real-life experience with 2,000 expert and entrepreneur authors, and takes you through the best planning and writing process you'll find for a book that will build your business. That real-life process has been gamified in the app, making the experience fun, full of 'Aha' moments and dopamine hits, along with the smartest time-savers, nudges and interventions that AI can offer.

But Book Magic AI will not write your book for you. What would be the point of that? (And no professional publisher will publish AI-generated content.)

Book Magic's brilliance is that I talk you through the entire process in this book, and the app will coach and support you in applying that learning. It will help you get your best ideas out of your head and onto the page, keep you accountable and take you through the emotional as well as intellectual journey of writing your book. Book Magic is here to showcase your expertise, experience, model, process, stories, case studies and uniqueness. The genius of Book Magic is to show that the real magic of your book is you!

SUSAN PAYTON, STORYTELLER

Susan Payton is a storyteller. Stories are her business, and her book is called *The Business of Stories.*

Even though Susan is an experienced storyteller and teaches others the art and craft of storytelling, she didn't feel she was experienced in the art and craft of writing a book.

She says that she put it off for a long time because she didn't know if she had anything unique to say.

> 'I felt like there were lots of books on storytelling. There were lots of people talking about storytelling, and I thought to write a book you had to have something that was completely different to what everybody else had. It had to be a really unique take or something ground-breaking, or just something that no one else was saying.'

Susan also felt under a lot of pressure to deliver a really, really good book because storytelling is how she is positioned in her market. She knew that if she put a book out into the world, she would want to feel confident that it was full of great stories, so there was added pressure for her.

Her third concern was that she didn't know if she had 35,000 words in her. Susan spends her time editing words down, making things concise and punchy, 'When I share stories I keep them short and simple, so the idea of writing 35,000 words was quite daunting, and I didn't know if I'd have enough to say.'

All of those things stopped Susan from moving forwards with her book project for a few years. Then when she looked at the Book Magic process, she was impressed and reassured that there was a structure to follow so she wouldn't be starting with a blank screen; there was a tried-and-tested process that had obviously been used by lots of other people. Susan thought, 'Well, a book is words, and I like writing words, and if I have a structure to follow and a bit of coaching to get me out of the blocks and make sure my initial outline is going to work, then I should be able to do this.'

Susan did write and publish her book. I'll be telling you more about her book journey as we continue through this book.

YOUR GOLDMINE

Humans have always been drawn to gold because of its visual beauty – its unique colour and shine, lustrous and metallic qualities, malleability and the fact that it doesn't tarnish. These, along with its relative scarcity and complex process of extraction, have made gold a consistently valuable commodity with an edge over other metals. The rarity and difficulty of mining gold has also meant no one could try to devalue the metal as a currency. As well as its aesthetic value, gold has a practical value – it is durable and non-corrosive, and it can be formed as needed for use in, among others, electronics, dentistry, medical tools, and the defence, aerospace and automotive industries.

Gold serves as a powerful metaphor for the knowledge economy, where your expertise and experience as a business leader, entrepreneur, coach, consultant or service provider is a precious commodity. Just as gold must be prospected, mined, extracted and refined, so too must your knowledge and experience be discovered, developed, articulated and polished to stand out in the marketplace. Your participation in this economy is not just about possessing valuable insights; it's about the ability to transform that intellectual capital into a tangible asset that can be shared, traded and leveraged for growth – much like the way gold is unearthed and processed to realise its full potential.

In *Book Magic*, I'm going to work with you to identify, reveal, refine and structure your precious knowledge and turn it into that iconic asset: a book. Just as a gold bar has a universal and recognisable format with accepted value, so too does a book. When you've worked through the process in these pages – and ideally supported by the Book Magic AI app – you will have turned your mine of raw gold into its purest, highest and most valuable form.

The gold on Earth originates in the depths of space, formed in cosmic events like supernovae and neutron star collisions. Gold atoms scatter through space via nuclear reactions and become incorporated into our planet's crust over billions of years. Gold formation takes place through geological processes like hydrothermal and magmatic activity and slowly accumulates in deposits over vast timescales – typically taking millions of years for minable gold deposits to form, making gold a precious and finite resource.

As an expert, founder, entrepreneur or business owner, you are standing on a goldmine of well-developed knowledge, experience and expertise. This is the content and intellectual property you are going to fill your book with. Luckily, your precious metal won't have taken millions or billions of years to develop, but it will have taken you time to accumulate the body of work that will show you to be the expert in your area. What should you have in your goldmine, and developed over what timeline, before you're ready to write and publish a book that will build your authority and your business?

Let's do a quick check.

YOUR BUSINESS

Think about your business, and ask yourself:

- Have you been operating for two years or longer?
- Do you have a well-defined product or service?
- Does your experience bring tangible benefits to your clients?
- Has your business been making a good annual profit for at least two years?

If the answer to three or more of these is 'no', it might not be the right time to write your book. Your gold stock might need a little more development before you start mining it for content. Taking some more time to work on your business, getting more experience with clients and defining your products and services more clearly will give you a better basis for the content of your book. While you're doing this, build your business profile and client base too.

Some startup founders and unicorns have had such a strong concept from the outset that they've written their book ahead of launching or consolidating their business, and built the business from the book up. While not the norm, this is not impossible and it might be your way forward.

But if you've answered 'yes' to two or more of these questions, you're nearly ready to write your book. In fact, taking the first step of identifying your market (your ideal client) and outlining a structure for your book will help you refine your business processes and better define your products and services. Stick with me.

If the answer to three or all of these questions is 'yes', your business is in great shape and your goldmine is bursting with value. You know your market, you have clearly defined products and services, and a proven process. Now would be an excellent time to write your book, serve your ideal clients and accelerate your business growth. You can use your book to raise your authority, generate more leads and boost your profile.

YOUR INTELLECTUAL PROPERTY (IP)

Your IP is part of your authority and will be a key source of the content for your book. Your book will consolidate your IP and when it's published, '© copyright *you*', it provides indisputable proof that you own the ideas it contains and created them first. Having your content and ideas published is the best way of protecting your valuable IP.

Don't worry about over-sharing and giving your prospects so much information that they won't need to buy your services, or your competitors the ability to steal your IP. The aim of your book is to give your prospects maximum information for them to see that they need to come to you for implementation – something the book can't offer. Making your IP or process public will mean anyone can see that it's yours and you can call out copyright theft.

So thinking about your IP, ask yourself:

- Have you built up a wealth of knowledge that offers people value?
- Have you been working in your specialist area for three years or more?
- Do you have a proven process, with clearly designated steps, that you work through with most clients?
- Do people ask where they can find out more about your work or regularly tell you that you should write a book?

If you've answered 'no' to three or more of these questions, your IP might not yet be clear or established enough to form the basis of an authoritative book. You may need to spend more time developing your expertise and in-depth knowledge before writing the book or creating an original piece of IP.

If you have answered 'yes' to at least one but can't be sure of two or more of the above, you still have valuable IP, and unpacking it through planning and writing your book could be an ideal way to mature, refine and protect it. The Book Magic AI app, or a real-life coach, will help you to clarify your processes, systems and procedures, and suggest models, tools and systems you can own. AI is great at supporting this kind of idea development.

With three or more 'yes' answers to these questions, you have well-defined, significant and original content based on a proven process of your own – pure gold. You are considered an expert in your field and clients seek you out. Now is the time to demonstrate your expertise more widely and protect what is yours by consolidating your IP through writing your business book.

YOUR CONTENT

Do you have enough original and high-value content already to form the basis of a successful business book? Ask yourself:

- Do you blog, write articles or create videos, podcasts or other content?
- Do you have case studies of clients or customers to illustrate your successful outcomes?
- Do you use your own story to inspire others and promote your business?

If none of the above apply to you, it would be a good idea to start building up some published content showing who you are, what you know and how you work, while you are working on your book. Create an archive of useful, interesting, unique content that serves your target audience and can be repurposed across the book and other media. The content you write now could form the basis for your book later.

Alternatively, start writing your book and repurpose your topics and stories as social media posts, talks or articles, and get early feedback on them. It works both ways. In fact, Book Magic AI can produce social media posts for all platforms, articles and blog posts, individually or in a series, at the touch of a key as you write sections of your book.

If you answered 'yes' to two of the questions above, you are already creating useful content, and getting your book project started will help you to spread your ideas more widely.

If you can say 'yes' to all of the above, you have most of the content you need to write your book. It's all part of your goldmine. Work through the Book Magic process to structure your content into a clear book format and you'll find that the writing will be easy.

Now let's get prospecting for your gold.

THE GOLDEN KEYS

Even with this book, the help of Book Magic AI and/or a real-life coach or writer, writing your book is a serious project and a journey that will have some emotional ups and downs. There will almost certainly be times when you wonder why you're putting yourself through this and whether it's worth it. Based on my experience, it's highly likely that at some point you'll suffer from (totally unwarranted) imposter syndrome and your inner critic will tell you that you have nothing interesting to say in your book and nobody will want to read it. This is entirely normal and most authors go through these stages, whether it's their first, second or umpteenth book – and most important: it's not real! You're likely just a bit tired, have come to a section that's harder to write or makes your brain ache, or need a bit of a break to process.

But when you do feel less than excited about your book project, it's helpful to remember what the glittering prizes will be when you get it done. These are the four golden keys that your published book will bring you:

1. Clarity and confidence
2. Authority and influence
3. Prospects and clients
4. Speaking and platforms

CLARITY AND CONFIDENCE

Every author I've worked with finds that the process of planning and writing their books is an amazing self-development exercise, both personally and professionally illuminating. Organising your thoughts, knowledge, experience and expertise into a detailed structure – the blueprint of a logical and enlightening journey for your reader – takes concentration but is always rewarding. It forces you to interrogate the steps of your process, your client or customer journey and the way you want to present your practice and your data to your readers.

Writing and editing your manuscript gives you the opportunity to unpack and review everything about your work and business. Sometimes it shows you how you can improve your process and your clients' journey; sometimes you get a sudden insight about that extra step you need to add in, or where you can simplify or clarify for your readers and clients; sometimes it helps you realise how to use your own stories or client case studies to sell your work and engage with new prospects. I've known quite a few authors get a flash of inspiration while writing about repositioning or pivoting their businesses – for the better and often the bigger.

Once you've written your manuscript, seen it all laid out and had it professionally edited, you will gain a new level of confidence in your own abilities and skills. Your book will have created an archive of content that you (or Book Magic AI) can repurpose into talks, blog posts, articles, podcasts, workshops, courses, presentations and keynotes. What's more, pitching, presenting, speaking and training all become easier when you've written your book. Through the writing process, you save all this content not only to your PC or the cloud, but also to the cloud drive in your head from where you can retrieve and repeat it at the drop of a hat.

AUTHORITY AND INFLUENCE

There is nothing that shows you're an authority or expert in your field like being the author of a published book. In an increasingly online environment, your printed book stands out as a physical product, representing you as well as containing your knowledge and skill in an iconic format. Added to which, your e-book is an electronic asset you can send to prospects, clients, colleagues and partners at the touch of a key. In addition, your audiobook speaks your own voice of authority directly into the ears of your listeners.

Your book's ability to go far and wide across continents, speaking to people you don't know and would never be able to contact, and being passed on through recommendations, reviews and online booksellers to ideal clients, is an extraordinary kind of influence and your second golden key to transforming your business.

Everyone respects an author, even more than you might imagine. In the world of entrepreneurs, lots of people talk about writing their book, but those who actually *finish* writing their books and get them published are still an elite minority. This makes us all the more valued and authoritative.

THE HR BUSINESS BOOK

Jill Aburrow is a qualified HR expert with thirty years' experience. Jill runs Heartfelt HR, providing small businesses with generalist HR advice, and also working directly with HR teams in larger companies to support their redundancy programmes. She wrote and published her first book, *Redundancy With Love: Getting it right for your people and your business* in 2023 and says that it has given her credibility in her industry.

Jill initially decided to write the book because she 'wanted employers to understand that there is a kind and compassionate way of dealing with redundancy, which brings better results for everyone involved.'

In showcasing her expertise in handling redundancies with compassion, Jill positioned herself as a trusted expert in the field of HR consulting. This strategic move increased her visibility, boosted her lead generation and enhanced her sales and repeat business. What's more, it significantly built her authority by:

- Differentiating her from other HR consultants: Jill is a redundancy expert, and she collaborates with employers who want to treat people with kindness and compassion. That's a strong brand. Having a book gives her the platform to showcase that brand,

so readers understand the values and approach they will be working with when they hire her or her firm.
- Building her confidence: The writing process teaches you a lot about your own expertise. As Jill says, 'It has proved to me and the world that I know what I am talking about.' That's precisely what building authority is about. Jill's book delivered an extra boost to her credibility and self-confidence when it was shortlisted for the Business Book Awards 2024.

By writing her book, not only was Jill able to convey her important message, but she also positioned herself as a leading authority in her niche.

Jill sends her book to current and potential clients and interested parties, often for free. In sharing it, she provides an opportunity for potential clients to learn more about the value of her HR consultancy services before they decide to buy. This approach allows her to establish a connection with her prospects, showcasing her expertise and insights more broadly and deeply than she could otherwise.

There's also a multiplier effect at play here. Jill's book has led to articles, podcasts and speaking engagements, which in turn have led to more leads and sales. Her book has also opened doors to new opportunities, such as media features and speaking engagements, which have further expanded her reach, influence and sales. Overall, the book has significantly enhanced her professional reputation and contributed to the growth of her consultancy business.

PROSPECTS AND CLIENTS

The third golden key that will come to you as a published author – and in terms of building your business it may be the biggest – is more and higher-value prospects and clients.

Everything you've invested, in terms of time and money, in getting your book written and published, will come back to you through your ideal clients seeking to work with you, as opposed to you having to hunt them down; through being able to attract more clients, better clients, clients paying you higher prices – because a key feature of a book is that it is not an obvious sales tool.

That's why we say that nothing sells you like a book and why we call it your 'undercover sales agent'. A book is not a business card, it's not a pitch, it's not a marketing brochure – all of which are well-known sales tools… and often end up in the bin. The gift of your book is an incredible tool to send out to prospects and clients, and will grow your business exponentially.

Your book is not out there saying, 'I am fantastic. This service is great. Here are my client testimonials. Here are my services and their prices.' You won't say any of that in your book. Your book is pure value. You are giving people the value that they are looking for – this comes with an actual price tag and many people will pay it, while others will receive and appreciate it as a valuable gift from you.

Your book is not a direct sales tool. It just tells people as a matter of fact, as a matter of value, what you do and how you do it. Because of the work you're going to do on the 3Ps of Position, you are going to aim it fair and square at your ideal clients, but this won't stop other people who are not in your specific target market from getting huge value from your book.

When you write your book and it is perfectly positioned for your market, it will draw them back to you and your services. It will magnetise them to come and work with you. Prospects and clients are who you are writing your book for – and what you will get as an outcome.

Your book also acts as a recruitment tool, telling prospective partners, service providers and colleagues what your values and vision are, how your business operates, how you work with clients and what will be expected of them if they want to be a part of your world.

SPEAKING AND PLATFORMS

Are you looking to raise your profile by getting speaking gigs, or more or better-paid or higher-profile speaking gigs? Writing and publishing your book will be your golden key to these engagements and to guesting on the best podcasts and featuring at industry events – everyone loves an author! Think about the experts and pundits we see on the media every day: almost inevitably, they're introduced as 'the author of…' Their book is the source of their authority to comment on their specialist subject. Not only does their book define their expertise, but it's likely how the programme producer or journalist found them in the first place.

Amazon has one of the most powerful search engines out there. If you have a book published on Amazon and someone searches for your name online, your book title or keywords in the description of your book, Amazon's algorithm ensures that you and your book will appear at the top of the search page. No book, no listing on Amazon.

While your area of expertise may or may not be of interest to the mainstream media, your local TV news, radio station and newspaper will love to interview you as a local author. Your own industry will also definitely be interested in getting you to speak, take part in panel discussions or run workshops, at home and potentially all over the world. However, you need to be proactive in finding the decision-makers and getting your book out and into their hands.

THE HOSPITALITY SUITE OF BOOKS

Monica Or has written three books on her niche in the hospitality industry. Her books cover all aspects of running a hotel business and working in the hospitality industry: *Star Quality Hospitality: The key to a successful hospitality business*; *Star Quality Experience: The hotelier's guide to creating memorable guest journeys*; and *Star Quality Talent: Inspiring hospitality careers*. She has consistently leveraged them to raise her profile and become the go-to expert in her field.

> 'From having my books published I have been invited to speak abroad at conferences, flown business class and had accommodation and expenses paid for as well as a speaker fee and large book orders. I have been paid to work with partners to run a Thought Leaders workshop, webinar and white paper. Content from my book has been turned into online courses. My status with my industry peers has been elevated and they now take me much more seriously. I have been interviewed for trade magazines and spoken at many conferences. It is now a lot easier to connect with people in my industry: many CEOs and managing directors are happy to meet with me and I can contact them directly without having to get past their gatekeepers!'

Monica's advice to authors is: 'Once your book is published, don't be shy, shout about it. Share your knowledge far and wide.'

BOOK MAGIC

Confidence, authority, influence, clients, income and speaking platforms are all transformational and predictable outcomes from writing and publishing your book. From my experience of mentoring and publishing thousands of entrepreneur authors' business books, I know that these are all results you can expect. Of course, you could publish your book and not tell anyone, not give or send it to any prospects or partners and basically do nothing with it. In which case, perhaps the effect will be minimal. However, if you think creatively about how you can use your book to achieve your goals, all of the above outcomes will be yours.

As well as these predictable outcomes, there are always some unpredictable results of publishing a great business book – results that sometimes seem almost magical. Some authors have found their book has put them in touch with their heroes; others have been invited onto high-powered committees, unexpectedly doubled their business, become media pundits, been flown across the world to speak – the sky's the limit!

BOOKS BUILD BUSINESS

Entrepreneurs and experts gain in three key areas when they write and publish a professional business or self-help book: impact, income and influence.

When you pitch to a prospect, walk into a first meeting with a client or turn up to a media interview, handing your book to the prospect, client or interviewer will double the impact you have on them. When you give a keynote and hand out free copies of your book, run a course in which the book is included as a resource, or simply reach into your bag and give a signed copy to a useful contact at a networking event, you are exponentially increasing your impact – on those people directly and all the others they talk to.

By far the greatest financial benefit to entrepreneur authors, and where they get the real return on their investment, is the high-level clients and contracts their books attract. Maybe you're finding it hard to move your business up a level from working with an established group of clients who know and like you to having prospects you don't even know approaching you for your services. When you craft your knowledge and processes into book form, they reach an audience you would never have the time or opportunity to contact personally. Your book becomes your ambassador, working twenty-four-seven to spread your name and expertise.

There is nothing like having authored a book to cement your credentials as a thought leader and authority in your market. Have you noticed how most media 'experts' are authors, how speakers and guests at events have at least one book to their name and how leaders in most industries are likely to have put their ideas into book form?

Now it's your turn to join that secret society: The Authors' Club.

THE £50,000 READERS

Marianne Page, business systems expert, wrote a first book called *Process to Profit* outlining her approach to systemising businesses for the benefit of owner entrepreneurs. Within six months, she had gained over £50,000 worth of contracts through just three people who read her book: a business owner who had picked it up on holiday and got in touch on his return, anxious to work with her; an old friend who heard Marianne had written a book so read it – and realised how much she could help him; and a franchisee who was recommended it and clocked that Marianne's system was just what he needed. Since then, she has written two more books, *Simple, Logical, Repeatable* and *Mission: To manage*, because each new book elevates her and her business to new levels of success.

Marianne Page is just one of many small business owners whose books have attracted business, whose prospects come 'pre-sold' on their ideas and want to pay high fees for implementation of a strategy they already understand and appreciate.

TWO
PROSPECTING

ORE, NUGGETS AND DUST

Armed with the knowledge of the benefits your book is going to bring you, let's get started on the process of creating your solid gold asset.

There are three types of gold we're going to prospect, mine, extract and refine from your business goldmine and turn into your book:

1. **Ore** represents the veins of solid value that underpin your business, starting with your robust client base. You may have a range of clients or customers who come to you to solve diverse problems and work with you in different ways. We are going to identify your ideal prospect, their typical issues and the solution you offer them – this will be the premise and promise of your book.

2. **Nuggets** of gold are rare and represent significant value, much like a well-established business model or process in an entrepreneur's arsenal. These are the tried-and-true methods that you have developed and honed, which your clients have found so effective and which now provide you with a unique service, reliable returns and the cornerstone for your business's ongoing prosperity and growth.

3. **Dust** is the other form of gold that a prospector sifts through the earth to find. You as an

entrepreneur have accumulated a wealth of industry knowledge over time. This knowledge might seem to you at the moment to be a collection of discrete pieces of data, experience, intuition and information, scattered throughout your business like individual flecks of gold dust. Collectively, these form a valuable asset that allows you to make informed decisions and strategic moves for your individual clients and within the wider market.

Prospecting is the first step in the mining process, and the ore, nuggets and dust in your goldmine are sitting there, waiting to yield their value to you.

There are different kinds of prospecting, though. Panning for 'placer' gold is a great start for chancers, popular since before the Gold Rush, and still a recreational activity in some countries like New Zealand, not unlike metal detecting in the UK. It's normally done with the same kind of pan that has been used for centuries to wash free gold particles from loose surface sediment. If placer gold is discovered by better-financed organisations, they will bring in sluices or mechanical devices to wash greater volumes of material. However, as the name 'placer' suggests, this is just a first step in trying to identify sites for more lucrative deep mining; what they're really looking for, by tracing the placers back to their sources, is hardrock gold deposits.

The prospecting we are going to start with is not about taking a chance on finding placer gold. The book equivalent of this would be doing some broad market research to identify potential interest in your products or services, to identify a subject for your book.

We don't need to look around for book ideas.

We know your hardrock or lode gold deposits are there. We're going to be drilling into a subsurface that you, through your business, have built up over years and writing the book that showcases your experience. We don't need to find placer gold to know that you're sitting on a goldmine full of ore.

This ore represents the deep, raw and perhaps unrefined potential within your business. For your book, it needs identifying, careful extraction and nurturing into content and case studies, and the conceptual tools we'll use to do this are as simple but effective as the mechanical diggers used for real gold.

We're going to approach the task of defining your ideal client, understanding their pain and crafting a promise to solve their problem with the meticulous care of a seasoned prospector searching for gold that they know is there. This is not a haphazard endeavour but a deliberate search for the individual whose needs align perfectly with the services or products you and your business offer. Your knowledge of your ideal client is the vein of gold that runs deep beneath the surface, waiting to be discovered by someone who knows where to look. You're going to sift through all your client experience and information and, much like the prospector, identify the glint of gold within the dirt and gravel.

So let's move on to our tried-and-tested tool – the 3Ps of Positioning.

But before we do, here's a snippet of information about another potential tool for prospecting. A 2012 study by Australian scientists found that termites have been found to excrete trace deposits of gold. According to the Commonwealth Scientific and Industrial Research Organisation in Australia, the termites burrow beneath eroded subterranean material that typically masks human attempts to find gold and ingest and bring the new deposits to the surface. They believe that studying termite nests may lead to less invasive methods of finding gold deposits. I'll let you know if we find the AI equivalent of termites for books.

THE FINANCE EXPERT'S BOOK

Landing new clients as a finance expert isn't without its obstacles. Prospects may have negative perceptions of your profession as a whole, due to past industry scandals or bad experiences with other advisers. Building trust in this field, when clients are often cautious about sharing personal financial information to begin with, takes skill, experience and strategy.

At the same time, you're handling the everyday challenges that come with the finance expert's role. You're navigating complex regulatory environments; you're ensuring your marketing materials comply with financial regulations; you're keeping up to date with changes in laws and industry standards.

Rob Gardner, investment consultant, entrepreneur and co-founder of RedStart, a charity for primary-school children that delivers financial education through progressive learning, wrote and published *Freedom: Earn it, keep it, grow it* in 2023. He initially decided to write his book because he had a mission: to help people achieve financial freedom in a world worth living in. 'This book has been transformational for getting out my message,' he says.

Rob used the 3Ps of Positioning to establish his **Person**: his book was aimed at young professionals. Their **Pain** was that, like so many people, they didn't understand how money works or how to make it work for them. The **Promise** of his book was that it would provide them with a simple toolkit to help them feel in control of their money, whether they were managing debt, saving for a rainy day or investing in their future.

Rob has a strong brand as an experienced financial adviser focused on financial education and sustainable investing so that money works for the planet as well as for the investor. Having a book gives him the platform to showcase that brand, so readers understand the values and approach they'll get if they work with him.

He has given 500 copies of *Freedom* away to teachers in the schools he's worked in with RedStart. It's a thoughtful and generous gesture – and it also turns some of those teachers into leads who might work with Rob in the future, or recommend him to people in their network. Rob has been particularly successful at using his book to do good. Not only does £2 from every copy go towards funding his charity, RedStart, but the book itself provides valuable financial education while establishing Rob's business credentials.

The fact that he's having this positive impact on the world also helps build trust, and may help to overcome any potential negative perceptions about finance experts.

3PS OF POSITIONING

You need to know just three things to get clarity and certainty about what book you should be writing now: I'll show you how to establish who your ideal client is – the 'Person' you're writing for; what their 'Pain' – their central question or problem – is; and how to make your book the answer or solution that will satisfy their needs and make them want to come to you for more – your big 'Promise'. This same information will enable you to come up with a great working title and subtitle.

The intersection between your ideal client and their central question defines your market. The intersection between your ideal client and your big promise is where you've positioned your business. The way you transform your client's central question into your big promise is your genius. Once you understand how these elements intersect, you have your book concept – a book that will appeal to your market, promote your business and be powered by your genius. Let's unpack it.

PERSON – YOUR IDEAL CLIENT

The important first step is to clarify exactly who you are writing your book for. Some authors with a broad subject matter can be tempted to say their book is for 'anyone and everyone'. Even a traditional publisher, looking for maximum retail sales, won't be happy with that answer – every book has to be sold from a section or shelf in a bookshop, or a handful of categories on Amazon. However, particularly for a business book author, who has other reasons for publishing than to achieve retail sales, it is best to focus on one or two ideal clients as the reader you are addressing.

To position your book to your market, consider:

- Your ideal client's business or type of business
- Their position in your/their industry
- Your ideal client's turnover or income (an amount below which they're unlikely to be able to afford your services)
- What their top three motivations for using your services would be

Try to define your ideal client's demographics – such as age range, gender and circumstances – and then give a name to a current, past or future ideal client. It can be helpful to create an avatar for them – the individual you would love to work with if you have a B2C business, or the decision-maker in a business you would most like as a client if you work B2B. They may be a theoretical concept at this point, or they could be someone you know but haven't made contact with yet, or someone who has already been your client and is the type of client you'd like to attract more of. Write a description, draw a picture or find an actual photo of this client, then keep it in your line of vision as you write your book as a one-to-one conversation with that person. This will also help you find your author voice when you start writing.

The AI in Book Magic AI leads you through this process brilliantly – it prompts you to give this and more information about your client base and then gives you an insightful and clear summary of what you've told it. What's more, it writes you an almost lyrical description of the way you and your genius serves your clients. A number of authors have told me they've almost been moved to tears by how the AI has shown them their true value. It also offers you images of your ideal client – some of which may make you laugh, but if you keep prompting it will almost certainly find one that you can write your book to.

Niching your book by writing to a single person won't restrict your audience – it will just help you to direct your information to the people most valuable to you, so they will want to come back and work with you. Other readers won't realise you've done this and will still feel you're talking directly to them.

PAIN – YOUR IDEAL CLIENT'S CENTRAL QUESTION

The second part of positioning your book is to establish the central question or problem that your ideal client avatar has. Ask yourself:

- What are your ideal client's biggest problems and what issues are they facing in their business or work?
- How do these problems impact them personally?
- What will happen if their problem persists?

To find these answers, write down the top three reasons your clients come to work with you, and the three most frequent questions your prospects and clients ask you.

Knowing and appealing to your ideal client's underlying problems tells you the position they will be in when they come looking for help through your book; the point in their business or personal journey at which you need to meet them with your solution. This is their central question.

Again, doing this in Book Magic AI gamifies the process so you're incentivised to get through it faster, focuses your responses and utilises all the information you input to help you throughout the book-writing journey.

PROMISE – YOUR BIG PROMISE TO YOUR READER

Third, ask yourself: what is your promise to your reader when they've read your book? Where will you have taken them to by the time they finish reading? What is the underlying solution that all your ideal clients will want you to provide?

To identify the answer, you need to unpack exactly how you improve your client's business, work or life. What is the unique solution that you offer your clients; how does it differ from other solutions or challenge conventional wisdom in your area? Write down the three top solutions or interventions you provide to the majority of your clients. List the benefits your readers or ideal clients will get if they take your advice or implement your solution. This is your big promise, and the subject matter of the book you should be writing right now to build your business.

Your book should be aimed squarely at the readership of your ideal clients, address the subject of their central question and provide the answer or solution with your big promise.

Whether you've done the 3Ps of Position exercise with pen and paper, in simple writing software or using Book Magic AI, I'm sure you'll have found it has brought you clarity and insight about your work, your business and – most importantly – the subject of your book. You will be writing your book for your Person, addressing their Pain points and showing how you deliver your big Promise that is the answer to their question, solution to their problem or healing to their pain.

You have gone prospecting for the gold that is your market and, from under the inevitable dirt, revealed the shining veins of ore that you are now ready to start extracting.

THE SPEAKER AND THE BOOK

Attracting more paid public speaking opportunities is a great goal to set yourself and your business: these opportunities bring in income, leads and kudos, as well as giving you great scope to develop your skills and your confidence. Many successful public speakers have found that having a book to their name has helped them net more and better speaking opportunities. Sarah Furness became a motivational speaker and leadership coach after twenty-one years as a combat helicopter pilot in the RAF, even though it wasn't her original plan. She published *Fly Higher: Train your mind to feel as strong as you look* in 2022 and says:

> 'I actually started out wanting to be a mindfulness coach. I wanted to show people there is a way through the darkest of times... but mindfulness is hard to sell and most of my prospects just wanted to hear stories about flying. Then I realised I could do both: I could teach techniques and tools rooted in mindfulness, and use combat flying stories to bring these techniques to life and prove that they work.'

Sarah initially decided to write a book to have something to hand out after her talks, but she quickly found that having a book helped her rise to many of the challenges of a public speaking business. As well as building credibility and marketing yourself as a speaker, you will also find, as Sarah did, that:

- A book is a huge upgrade from a business card. When you meet new people, you can give them a copy of your book. You can give your existing clients several copies to give to their friends. Giving books away is a valuable and memorable way to build your network.
- If you struggle to stand out in a crowded market where many speakers vie for the same opportunities, a book helps set you apart.

- Having a book gives you the opportunity to showcase your brand so readers understand what they'll get when they hire you to speak.

Nothing sells you like a book. It's a more in-depth marketing tool than an ad or an email campaign, and more efficient than arranging multiple face-to-face meetings. Sarah Furness offers her book to new prospects to help her close speaking deals, giving potential clients a chance to see the value of her offering before they book her and making that booking more likely.

In 2024, Sarah published *The Uni-tasking Revolution: Focus on what really matters, get stuff done, waste less time* and she uses both her books not only as follow-up tools after speaking engagements, but also as thank-you gifts for referrals. It's a thoughtful approach, showing appreciation for those vital referrals and providing a tangible reminder of Sarah's insights and stories, making it more likely that people will come back to her again and again for speaking events and/or to work with her in other ways. Sarah's books are more than marketing tools: they are key to her client retention strategy.

TITLE AND SUBTITLE

Before we leave the 3Ps of Position, there's one other critical function they provide in positioning your book to your market. These three crucial axes – Person, Pain and Promise – determine not only the subject of the book you need to write, they are also your guide to creating a compelling title and subtitle for your book that will tell your market that your book is for them, and they need to read it now.

Between them, your title and subtitle need to address all three Ps: to tell your ideal reader that your book is specifically for them; to show them that you understand their problem; and to draw them into reading it because the front cover summarises your promise to them. Here are some tips on how to nail your title and subtitle.

SUMMARISE THE 3PS

Start creating your title and subtitle by quickly and intuitively writing one-sentence summaries of:

- Your ideal client (Person)
- Their central question (Pain)
- Your big promise (Promise)

Look at the words you've chosen and decide which are the most impactful and engaging. Write each word on its own card or Post-it note and move them around, adding linking words.

EIGHT KEY CONSIDERATIONS

Bear in mind the following eight considerations as you select the keywords for your title and subtitle:

1. A good title is like a good headline, so model newspapers and magazines.
2. Your title's number one job is to make people want to open the book.
3. Make your title dramatic by using powerful, active and emotive words.
4. Make a big promise or say something shocking or provocative.
5. Ask a leading question to make prospective readers curious.
6. Pose a conundrum that will engage your audience.
7. If you have a clever, witty or cryptic main title then your subtitle must explain your book's big promise.
8. Don't try to be clever if a more obvious title is stronger and more engaging.

TWENTY POWER WORDS OR PHRASES

Including any one or a combination of these words can power up the impact of your book title and subtitle:

- How to
- Secrets of
- Stop
- Start
- Discover
- Unleash
- Change
- Never
- Always
- Overcome

- Unlock
- Beat
- Free
- You/your
- Ways to
- The key to
- The secret to
- Master
- Become
- Learn to

NO NUMBERS

Even if your book is based around your five-step, six-key or four-point model, there is little value in making those numbers part of your main title. Remember that your title/subtitle combination has to contain as many keywords as possible, words that your ideal clients might use to search for a solution to their problem. No one ever searched for 'the five steps to…' to solve their problem or answer their central question, so don't waste three or four words out of the twelve to twenty you have available.

Also, never use a number in place of a word in a title just so that it matches a website address or product name. 'For' is not the same as '4' and 'to' is not the same as '2'.

PUTTING ALL THE PIECES TOGETHER

Spend some time coming up with a few titles and subtitles. Mix and match them. Play around with word order. Make sure you don't repeat any words in the title or subtitle, as you want to make maximum use of every keyword.

If you're working in Book Magic AI, you can ask the AI to come up with suggestions for both titles and subtitles. You can keep prompting and it won't get bored! Your own final version will most likely be better and more intuitive than most of the AI suggestions, but it will give you new ideas, come up with words you hadn't considered and different phraseology to your own. Remember that AI is likely to be more simplistic and clichéd than you. It has access to more information out there on the internet than you would ever have time to read, but it can't get to the one place most of your gold is buried: inside your head.

Make sure you are positioning your book as a positive solution. This means focusing more on your big promise than your ideal client's central question or problem. *Book Magic: Become an author faster and transform your expertise into business gold* is more engaging (I hope) than *How Not to Write the Wrong Book*, for example. The subtitle speaks with authority by using the imperative tense, summarises the promise to 'become an author faster' and refers to the metaphor of goldmining that I'm using throughout the book.

When you've come up with a few ideas, whittle them down to three titles and three subtitles. Mix and match them, then try them out on a few close associates – colleagues and current clients, or even prospects that you have a relationship with, are ideal. Your tribe on social media is not – it's too soon to go public with your book concept.

Combined, the title and subtitle should clearly indicate what the book is about and flag to your ideal client that it is aimed squarely at them, focusing on your big promise. It should be easy to spell, pronounce, remember and share, and finally, don't try to be too cryptic or clever. If it's not immediately obvious what the book is about and who it's for, it becomes like a bad joke – not funny if you have to explain it.

Here are three examples of effective titles and subtitles:

1. *From Learner to Earner: A recruitment insider's guide for students wanting to achieve graduate job success,* by Sophie Milliken. Sophie Milliken's ideal client is a graduate student, demonstrated in the use of keywords 'students' and 'graduate'. Their central question is 'How do I get a good

job after university or college?' And Sophie's big promise is contained in the dynamic main title, the journey from being a learner to an earner, and in the subtitle wording 'achieve graduate job success'. She also includes her own credentials as the author in the phrase 'a recruitment insider's guide'.

2. *Impact: How to be more confident, increase your influence and know what to say under pressure*, by Dominic Colenso. Dominic's ideal client is clearly someone who either is or wants to be an expert communicator and speaker. Their central question is around how they can increase their confidence when communicating with others and use their platforms to become more influential. Dominic's big promise is superbly condensed in the single word 'impact' – everything his ideal client wants to have. He then speaks to the characteristics his readers want to feel and embody: confidence, influence and the ability to find the right words even in stressful situations.

3. *Pull Back Your Power: The ground-breaking code to unlocking profound confidence and soaring success for aspirational women*, by Anne Whitehouse PhD. Anne's ideal client is a woman either in business or with ambition to succeed in her career. As a scientist herself, who had experienced sexism in academia, she wanted to include all ambitious women, so she used the word 'aspirational' rather than 'business' or 'professional'. Her

market's central question relates to lack of confidence and high stress, leading to loss of wellbeing and less successful career outcomes, and her big promise is in her analytical research – hence the word 'code' and the 'PhD' after her name. Her big promise is to help women feel safe and truly entitled to shine ('profound confidence'), enabling them to take off and fly high ('soaring success'). 'Pull Back Your Power' relates to Anne's key mind-training exercise in the book and also summarises her big promise to women.

Interestingly, though Anne's book is aimed at her ideal client, she told me she has also received heartfelt thanks from women who have been empowered to leave personal situations of domestic violence or coercive control after reading her book. This goes to show that even if your book is targeted directly at your ideal client, many others will also find value in it.

THREE
MINING

THE GOLD IN YOUR IP

Gold, like knowledge, has been a valuable currency throughout human existence.

Although gold shares many properties with other precious metals, such as silver and platinum, it is unique in others. The colour, lustre and density of gold, when it has been extracted from the ground, refined and shaped into anything from gold bars to jewellery to works of art, are just some of the qualities that set it apart from and allow it to command the highest price among other metals. Its value also lies in the fact that people have always been willing to accept it in exchange for something else. Supply and demand is a human constant, and gold is no exception. Governments, banks and individuals have used the noble metal as a store of wealth and a means of exchange for millennia.

From the time humans started trading with the abstract concept of 'money', the physical properties of gold have made it the ideal metal for use as currency. It is non-reactive, portable, non-toxic and fairly rare. This description also perfectly fits the IP you've built up yourself and in your business. There was enough gold to create plenty of coins, but it was scarce enough that not everyone could find it and make their own gold coins. Gold's unique characteristics also mean it cannot be manufactured or counterfeited; nothing compares to the real thing – again, just like your knowledge and experience.

While gold was initially valuable due to its societal status when used for jewellery and coins, it later developed industrial applications that have given it an additional inherent value – and yet its practical applications aren't so many that it is consumed by, for example, industrial demand, unlike steel. It is stable and virtually indestructible, but not so intractable that it can't be easily melted down and worked into other artefacts.

Despite the ending of the Gold Standard in 1971, by which gold provided a basis for international trade, national central banks and other large financial institutions still hold many metric tonnes of gold reserves as a physical store of wealth. On the financial markets, over long periods, gold investments hold their value, even while other assets like stocks crash, so gold provides a long-term safe haven and is a useful hedge or counterbalance against other investments.

Your knowledge, experience, expertise and unique applications of these – your IP – operate in the business market much like gold does in the financial markets. They have high intrinsic value, but the perception of their value, and the use that other people can make of them, is far greater when they are packaged into a simple, recognisable, exploitable format that acts as a means of exchange. When your process or model for your clients is something that they can see at a glance will add value to their business, it commands a higher price. In that form, it is a long-term commodity that they will want to pay you for, first for the information you provide in your book, and then for the implementation you can offer through your services. The process of mining your golden IP and shaping it into a book-shaped gold bar will transform it into the purest and most saleable version of your value.

Now that you've prospected for a clear concept for your book, worked towards an engaging and descriptive title and subtitle (which doesn't have to be finalised until you finish writing) let's move on to mining your gold.

How gold is mined depends on the type of deposit that can be found. There are two main types: placer and lode deposits.

1. **Placer deposits** – accumulations of loose gold in the sediments of a stream bed or a beach – are the easiest to mine. Miners scoop up sand, gravel and rock, mix it with water and use a metal or plastic pan to separate the gold from under the sediments. Hence the phrase, 'panning for gold'.

2. **Lode deposits** are concentrations of gold found in solid rock. For surface level gold-bearing rock, open-pit mining involves drilling holes that are filled with explosives to break up the ground so it can be loaded into haul trucks and taken to be separated. Deeper lode deposits need shafts and tunnels drilled for the explosives to reach the ore.

We are going to start by mining your easy-to-access placer deposits of IP to create the summary overview of your book. You'll be able to use this even before the book is written, for your own clarity and as useful information for others, and – with tweaks – as the Introduction at the start of your manuscript when you've finished writing.

We'll be digging deeper for lode deposits when we move on to creating the deep and detailed structure. This will be your blueprint, and I suggest you don't start writing until it is solid and in place. This may be harder work, but I promise you no explosives will be needed.

THE FIVE-STEP BOOK INTRODUCTION

Now you've thought about what will attract and retain your ideal readers' attention, how you will demonstrate your understanding of their problems and gain their trust, and now that you've created an ideal client avatar and know what help they need from you in your book, it's time to take the first step in externalising your work onto the page.

The Introduction to your book is the first thing your reader will see when they open your book, so you need to get it right. A good Introduction is short and sharp – it's not a chapter and it's not a place to tell your life story. You can write the perfect Introduction to your book in five short paragraphs of about 250 to 300 words each. This needs to be written by you in the first person – think of it like you're entering a room and meeting a prospect for the first time, introducing yourself in a personal but professional way and demonstrating that you understand them, and that they can trust you. Although I'll break it down for you into five discrete paragraphs, you can turn it into flowing, easy-to-read copy that makes your reader want to jump straight into your book and find out how you can help them.

PARAGRAPH I – WELCOME AND DESCRIBE YOUR IDEAL CLIENT

Start by describing your ideal client – the person you are writing this book for. If you can turn the notes you have made on your Person from the 3Ps of Position into a 250–300-word description, your ideal client (and ideal reader) will see that this book is for them. They need to know that you are speaking to them directly, so the first section should enable them to identify themselves as part of the community, however wide or specific, you and your book will bring value to.

You've already created an ideal client avatar from the first P of position, so just expand on this. You can check the Introduction to this book if you want to see how I've put this into practice. Also, because you are my ideal client, I'd love to know whether my first paragraph nailed it for you and made you feel that this book was the right place for you to be. Feel free to let me know!

PARAGRAPH 2 – INTRODUCE YOURSELF AS THE AUTHOR AND EXPERT

The next section should then position you as the expert author. Here, you want to tell your ideal reader how you work with people like them, along with highlighting key aspects of your expertise and experience that will show them they can trust you to solve their problem. If you're not sure how to pitch yourself for this role, the AI in Book Magic AI will give you a glowing summary from the information you've already given it. Remember that you can't copy and paste AI-generated text into your actual manuscript; you will need to rewrite any content in your own words, but I think you'll agree, it gives you a great starting point.

PARAGRAPH 3 – DESCRIBE YOUR IDEAL CLIENT'S PROBLEMS AND EXPLAIN WHY YOU CARE

The third section is where you describe your reader's problem – their Pain from the 3Ps of Position. This is the reason they are reading your book. Demonstrate to them in this paragraph that you understand what they are experiencing and that you empathise with their situation. Remind yourself what your ideal client wants to achieve in their business or their life, what challenges and problems are stopping them from reaching their goals and what will happen if their problem persists. Knowing and appealing to your ideal client's underlying problems tells them that you understand where they are when they pick up your book looking for help – the point in their business or personal journey they're at, and where you are ready to meet them with your solution.

PARAGRAPH 4 – OUTLINE THE BENEFITS YOUR IDEAL READER WILL GET FROM READING YOUR BOOK

This part is all about your Promise. Summarise the promise of your book to your readers so they feel secure in the knowledge that reading your book will solve their problem or answer their question. This paragraph is not about the content of the book, but about the results that reading your book will bring the reader. Don't outline what you're going to be telling them chapter by chapter, just tell them, in

250–300 words, the positive outcomes you're going to bring them.

What is the underlying and detailed solution that all your ideal clients will want you to provide? To define this for them and for yourself, you need to unpack exactly how you can improve their business, work or life. What is the solution that you offer your clients, and how does it differ from other solutions or challenge conventional wisdom in your area? List the benefits your readers or ideal clients will get if they take your advice or implement your solution. Give them a taste of the value they will derive and make them anxious to read on and get the benefits of your knowledge and experience.

PARAGRAPH 5 – INTRODUCE THE UNIQUE PROCESS YOU'RE GOING TO TAKE YOUR READER THROUGH

Finally, the content of your book will be based on your original vision that has created your unique service, product or concept. What is the process, overarching model or framework you take all your clients through? If you haven't already, summarising it in this paragraph is a chance to standardise and develop it into defined steps.

To finish up, give them a taste of what makes your book original. Here you can spend your last 250 words or so briefly talking about your process or model, or something intriguing about your own journey, or perhaps mention a client you got some amazing result for...

And that's it! If you follow that five-paragraph outline in that order you'll have the perfect 1,200–1,500-word Introduction to your book. This piece of writing will also be incredibly useful as a summary before your book is finished, or as a pitch, or even the basis of a press release. Get it written now and you'll find it helps you hold your book's overview in your head as you go through the writing process.

MY STRUCTURE STORY

As a writer and author, I have worked in many genres and formats over the years. I've been a journalist and reviewer; I've written TV scripts and treatments; business and research reports and manuals; self-development books and novels, and seven books (including this one) on how to write books. I'm also an editor and publisher who has worked on manuscripts, and with authors of all kinds. I'm obsessed with the importance of structure in books and stories, but this wasn't always the case. In fact, the reason I came to learn and understand how vital structure is came about through my own ignorance.

Even though I'd always wanted to write fiction, I didn't attempt to write a novel until I was about forty and felt that I might have enough life experience to create a story that filled 80,000 or so words. My first draft was a thinly disguised tale of part of my own life, around the theme of biological and adopted families and whether blood was thicker than water. At that point, I'd written a couple of non-fiction books about work–life balance (hard to believe, but this was a new concept at the time!) and both times I'd been given specific briefs by the publisher. I was determined that my novel was going to be all creativity, flow and originality.

Without any clear idea of where it was going, I poured my story out onto pages of manuscript, loved the process and thought I'd written something really special. I sent it to an agent I knew, who came back to me within two weeks – how exciting, she must have loved it! But her letter told me my story was (a) boring and (b) unbelievable.

'But it can't be unbelievable,' I whined. 'It's true!'

'Truth and fiction are not the same thing,' she snapped. 'Your story has no plot, no structure and that makes it unsatisfying to the reader.'

When I'd stopped sulking, I realised she was right. I went away and read everything I could about book structure, plot and planning. I studied what lies behind good fiction and non-fiction. I completely rewrote my novel, entered it in the inaugural Richard and Judy 'Search for a Bestseller' competition, where it was shortlisted from 47,000 entries, and *Blood and Water* was published by Macmillan New Writing.

From then on, structure and planning have been the cornerstone of my writing – fiction and non-fiction – and of the mentoring work I do with other authors. Although the art and creativity of writing are important in any book, it's just as important to understand the craft – even science – of book writing, and to make that the basis of your book planning and writing process.

THE MAGIC BOOK PLAN

I've developed and refined our unique Book Magic book planning system over more than ten years through working with around 2,000 entrepreneur and expert authors. To begin with, we would work in person with authors using coloured index cards to plan their books. Then we created standalone book planning software that we used with individual clients, and now the process has been elegantly incorporated within the Book Magic AI app. This is by far the best place to plan your book, but if you prefer to work on your kitchen table or the floor, one pack of white index cards and one pack of four colours (pink, blue, green and yellow) of index cards still works just as well.

Unlike most book planning formulae, this method starts not from the top down, but from the bottom up. Of the five colours of cards, the first three represent three vital types of content you need in your book; the last two colours are to help structure your content into chapters and parts. This will create a strong but flexible book structure that the majority of business books – books designed to build their author's business – will fit into. If it looks complicated at first glance, don't worry. I'm going to deconstruct it for you so you can create your own book structure in a series of simple steps.

There are two possible starting points, depending on how clear you are at this point on the structure that your book will follow. If you already have a pretty good idea, particularly if you have a model or framework that describes your process and will underpin the structure of your book (eg steps will be chapters), it may be best for you to start with the pink cards for chapter headings rather than thinking about individual topics, and populate your chapter cards with topics later. If you don't yet have a fixed idea about how your book will take shape, for most authors no matter where you're up to, I advise starting with the white card or line topics. I'm going to refer to 'cards' from now on, although in the Outline view in Book Magic AI, these appear as coloured lines.

WHITE CARD 'TOPICS'

The first thing we need to think about are the 'Topics'. On white cards, or when creating white (or slightly grey) lines in Book Magic, write the individual topics that you need to cover in your book, immediately as they come to mind, as many as you can think of. These should be topics that you want to tell your ideal client/reader about throughout the process of working with you. Each one should represent a blog-post-type piece of between 500 to 1,000 words. On each line or card, write just a heading for a topic, no detail.

Do this fast and intuitively. Don't stop to think about which order they should come in, how much you need to say about each, or whether you will need to research some topics. Just create the line or pick up a card and write. When you have thirty to forty topic headings, you have created the main body of your book content.

BLUE CARD 'STORIES'

The next step is to create 'Story' content, on blue cards or lines. These stories will intersperse and illustrate your factual topics, and be drawn from your own practical experience.

The two most important types of story are short case studies, little vignettes of successful interventions with your own clients, written as practical illustrations of your white topics, and anecdotes about parts of your own business or personal journey, both successes and failures, ups and downs. Sharing these stories will engage your ideal client and reader in a different way than your factual content. They will allow them to see that you and your clients have experienced the same challenges as they are facing now, and that you know how to solve their problems in real-life situations. Case studies can also include excerpts from interviews with clients, colleagues, partners or quotes taken from your own research.

Each story heading represents around 250–300 words of narrative that will give your reader an insight into you personally and your work on the ground. These are what I call your 'undercover sales agents' that draw ideal clients back to work with you. Every ideal client reading your book should be able to identify so strongly with three or four case studies that they will immediately want to get in touch and ask you to help them in the same way. Ten to twenty blue card stories should be about the right amount, scattered consistently through the book. It's not a good idea to put all your case studies together at the end of the book; they're much more powerful used individually to demonstrate different parts of your process. It's also best not to start the book with your entire personal back story; again, take relevant excerpts from your own learning journey to show the reader how you used to be like them but have successfully moved forward and now have the resources and experience to help them through the same problem.

GREEN CARD 'DATA'

Next is 'Data'. On green cards, we're looking for supporting evidence to prove, rather than illustrate, your white topics. These could be quotes, references, ideas, models, research and content from other experts that have inspired you, that have contributed to your own work, model or process, and that would be important to reference or useful to point your reader to. This can also be drawn from your own original research. Data can include books, articles, statistics, facts, figures, graphs, charts, tables – all of these will flesh out your white factual topics in a different way, and give support and substance to your views. Remember that other people's work, whether quotations, references or images, must be attributed and referenced, and in some cases needs permission to reproduce. You will need to check all of this with your publisher or editor, but it's always good practice to note down sources as you go along – it's much harder to go back and hunt down the right reference later.

PINK CARD 'CHAPTERS'

Now it's time to create 'Chapters'. The nature of books is that they are read line by line, page by page and chapter by chapter. Now that you've identified headings for all three types of content your book should include, you need to put your white, blue and green headings into a logical order under sequential chapter headings on pink cards or lines. Think about the order in which you want to take your reader through the information you're giving them, and start grouping the content cards accordingly.

Then, on pink cards (or lines), write the number and title of the chapters that will contain your white card content and blue and green card illustrations/evidence. Between six and twelve chapters is ideal: fewer than six makes for rather long chapters; more than twelve results in short chapters. If your model or process is clearly defined, the steps should all be chapter headings.

You can either start with chapter headings and populate them, or sort existing white, blue and green cards into chapters and then come up with a heading. Keep it consistent. All your chapters should have a similar amount of white topics within them – these will provide subheadings within your chapters – and the blue stories and green data should be scattered consistently through the chapters, illustrating and supporting the white topics.

YELLOW CARD 'PARTS'

In a final step, you may (or may not) want to sort your chapters into overarching 'Parts' – a minimum of two and a maximum of four. Three is ideal. Or you may not – this book doesn't have overarching parts; chapters are the top line structure.

If it works for your book, on yellow cards or lines, you can divide your chapters and their contents into overarching parts. The parts might represent beginning, middle and end, or theory, model and implementation. You also need to add 'Introduction' and 'Conclusion' – these are not parts or chapters. Every book needs a start and a finish.

In the flexible Book Magic planning system, you could have started from the bottom up with white card topics, added blue stories and green data, then sorted them into pink chapters and finally divided the chapters into yellow parts. Or you could have started with chapter headings, populated these with the three different types of content, then divided them up into parts. Or you could even have worked from the top down, starting with the overarching parts, breaking them down into chapters and finally populating the chapters with the white, blue and green card content.

YOUR BOOK BLUEPRINT

In Book Magic AI you can choose between the Outline view – a contents page of coloured lines; the Planner view, which looks like index cards and works particularly well for brains that like a 3D view or more kinetic format; or Text view, where you will see your contents page followed by the whole manuscript.

In any view, this is your book blueprint. It will allow you to keep an overview of your book structure in front of you as you write and tackle it as a 'writing by numbers' exercise. With every element of your content listed out, your first draft will be about filling in the blanks. From the titles of your 250-word case studies to your 1,000-word topics, writing this initial draft will consist almost entirely of simply getting your existing knowledge out of your head and onto the page – not necessarily even in chronological order.

Here is a summary list of all the elements you could or should include in your final (not first draft) manuscript (* = optional):

1. **Front matter** – 1,000 words

    - Praise quotes (about six to twelve short paragraphs over two pages – they must be about the book, not you or your business or services)*
    - Copyright/imprint page (usually provided by your publisher)

- Contents page
- Dedication (short, usually to family members or others who inspire you)*
- Foreword (500 words, written by someone else)*

2. **Introduction** – 1,200–1,500 words

    - Who your book is written for
    - Who you are
    - The problem you've written your book to solve
    - Your book's big promise to the reader
    - Short summary of the journey the reader will go on

3. **Part One*** (eg Beginning, Status Quo or Theory)

    - Includes two to five chapters, up to 10,000 words
    - Each chapter contains three to five topics, illustrated consistently with case studies, anecdotes, research, references, etc

4. **Part Two*** (eg Middle, Main Content or Model)

    - Includes two to five chapters, up to 10,000 words
    - Each chapter contains three to five topics, illustrated consistently with case studies, anecdotes, research and references, etc

5. **Part Three*** (eg End, Implementation or Outcomes)

    - Includes two to five chapters, up to 10,000 words

- Each chapter contains three to five topics, illustrated consistently with case studies, anecdotes, research and references, etc

6. **Conclusion/Summary** – 500 to 1,000 words
   - Main points of your book
   - What the reader now knows
   - What the future holds for them
   - What they should do next (contact you, further free info…)

7. **Back matter** – 1,000 words
   - References/Further Reading*
   - Acknowledgements (thank anyone and everyone who has helped get your book inspired, written and published)
   - The Author (300-word bio ending with your website, social media contact details and a hi-res black-and-white headshot)

The total word count you should be aiming for with a business book is typically around 35,000.

SUSAN PAYTON, STORYTELLER

Susan Payton, author of *The Business of Stories*, says that the initial work on the structure of her book, outlining the chapters and their contents and making sure there were enough stories included, made all the difference to being able to write it successfully.

'The different coloured cards and the format for planning with them was all so helpful, and I know it created the right outcome because the final published book works really well. I've had so much feedback over the years about what a great format it is, how easy it is to follow and how consistent and logical it is. Readers like that going through my book is a process – it's a process that people enjoy and they can get into a rhythm with it because of the structure.'

Susan says that being coached through the Book Magic approach to creating her book outline, and also writing the Introduction upfront, was really helpful.

'I probably wouldn't have started with that of my own accord. I would likely have assumed that you'd write the Introduction at the end when you're sure of what's in the book. Even though it did change, and I tweaked it as I wrote, writing the Introduction first helped to set the scene and made me think about the journey I wanted to take people on, what that would look like and what I wanted them to take from it. It made a massive difference. There's no way I would have got the book finished in the time that I got it done in, and I don't think it would've come out anywhere near as good, well thought through, laid out and structured as it did, without that initial planning and structural work.'

FOUR
EXTRACTING

SEPARATING GOLD FROM ORE

We've been prospecting in your goldmine for your ideal client and your book premise aimed at that person. We've mined the surface gold for your book Introduction, and dug deeper for the hardrock ore that has provided the detailed structure of your book blueprint. Now we're going to extract the gold from that ore through the process of writing your book.

After mining, the ore is usually crushed and ground and then there are a variety of methods for extracting the gold from the ore, such as amalgamation – wetting and dissolving gold in mercury to form an amalgam to create small gold particles; cyanidation – dissolving gold in an alkaline cyanide solution; centrifugation – separating gold particles from a concentrate in a centrifuge, where gold is caught in ridges while lighter materials are ejected; and magnetic separation – separating iron oxide minerals from copper and gold.

While you're not going to need physics or chemistry to extract the pure gold content of your book, the first step of the WRITER Process, Write (your first draft), is an incisive way of separating out the golden information that will provide the highest value information to your readers – your ideal clients – from the other solid experience you have, and will use in other places, but isn't crucial to the content of your book.

But first let's look at four tools that could equate to crushing and grinding your ore in advance of serious extraction.

YOUR AUTHOR MINDSET

A great starting point for your extraction process is to adopt a mindset based on another acronym: AUTHOR, which stands for Attention, Understand, Trust, Help, Order and Reaction. If you focus on these elements in advance of and while writing your manuscript, you will find yourself in a heightened state of awareness. New ideas will float up from the archive of your subconscious and also from books you read, your work colleagues and clients, and things that people say. What reaches you from the media (social and otherwise) will seem to crackle with relevant facts, figures, information and links that you can add into the mix of your first draft.

Writing a book is not just about the time you spend typing at your keyboard with your eyes on your screen (or writing in a notebook, if you prefer old-school tools). It is also about all the times in between, when your mind is consciously and unconsciously reviewing, sifting, connecting and shaping the knowledge you have into the elements of your book. It's a state of mind you enter for the period of the writing process, and an awareness of how to leverage this state of mind will help you create an inspirational book.

It is common to talk about the two kinds of processing our brains carry out: Buddhism characterises them as intellect and intuition, Carl Jung as conscious and subconscious, Daniel Kahneman as thinking fast and thinking slow. However you want to describe them, we have overt, aware thought-processing that deals with instant problems and questions, does active planning and organising, logical analysis and decision-making, keeps short-term dates and times in mind and works during your waking hours; and we have covert, opaque concept-processing that carries out more complex functions like meeting deadlines, finding solutions to intractable problems, germinating new ideas, linking events and concepts, retrieving buried information from our mental archive and 'composting' books and other projects, without our conscious involvement.

When you step into the world of writing your book, you can engage your intuition, subconscious or thinking fast in an active way to expand your thought development. If you purposefully set your subconscious to work on both general creativity and specific tasks, it will take up the challenge and save you lots of conscious work and hard thinking time.

Use the AUTHOR framework for your own benefit while you write:

- Pay **A**ttention to the work your subconscious can do for you by planning ahead. Decide on the subject of a writing session the day before, make a note of the title and tell your subconscious to prepare. Then don't do any conscious preparation work for it. You'll be surprised at how much information comes into your mind when you start and how much smoother your writing time is than if you were starting from scratch.
- **U**nderstand your personal preferences and styles for thinking, planning, organising and meeting deadlines; consciously use your strengths and mitigate any weaknesses for the benefit of this task.

- Trust your reticular activating system. This is the part of your brain that acts as a gatekeeper to your conscious awareness, and protects you from overwhelm by filtering out the unnecessary and less important aspects of life. If you train it to focus on book-related information, you will begin to find that useful data and connections from all sources appear as if by magic in your mental inbox.

- Ask for Help when you need it, from those around you at home and at work – you might need them to cut you some slack, especially while you're writing your first draft. Professional help could make the difference between a good book and a great book that will transform your business.

- Maintain Order in your thoughts and your writing. Stick to writing from your detailed book plan, whether that's on cards or in Book Magic AI. The app makes it easy to do this as in Outline view, you just click on each title, write your content in the editor, then close and move on to the next. You can choose to do this in chronological order or not. Create your writing habit (coming up shortly) and stick to it.

- Anticipate the positive Reaction your book will earn and the value it will bring to more people than you can imagine. Plan for the constructive effect it will have on your ideal clients and picture your enjoyment of the unexpected reactions from them and further afield – the ones we call Book Magic.

RESEARCH

Research is a great way to get either supportive or original content for your book. Just to remind you, there are two kinds of research: primary research and secondary research. Primary research you do directly with your subjects; secondary research is looking up existing material in books, reports, journals, websites etc, that other people have already explored, analysed, tested and written about, and that you can quote and reference. In many books, it's important to have secondary research to show that you have read around your subject and know what you're talking about, and to reference other people's work as well as your own to support your assertions. Ideally, you want a bit of both primary and secondary research in your book.

You might want to consider increasing or consolidating your unique and original content by doing some primary research on your specific market or subject matter. There are two kinds of primary research:

Quantitative research produces facts, figures and hard data. This comes from asking 'closed' questions in surveys or questionnaires, meaning the questions are designed to have binary (yes/no, 1/0, tick/cross), multiple choice or numerically ranked answers. You can analyse this data and discuss the results in your text; you can display the results as illustrative data (green lines in Book Magic AI) in bullet pointed lists, percentages, averages, graphs, charts and tables. Closed questions with pre-coded response options are ideal for researching topics where you know what kinds of responses you need to support and illustrate the points you're making in your book.

Quantitative research requires a reasonable number of responses to a survey or questionnaire to make the outcomes and conclusions you can draw from them credible, or 'statistically significant'. There's no fixed number that makes your research statistically significant – it depends on the context and the nature of the sample market you are surveying. If you have a niche market, a small pool of responders to your survey can still give useful data.

Qualitative research captures personal responses based on experience, beliefs, opinions and behaviour. Qualitative research is conducted using the answers to 'open' questions recorded or written in interviews, focus groups and surveys, where you ask participants to give reasons for or expand on their views on a 'closed' response, or standalone questions or discussions. You can do this by email, on calls that you record and transcribe, in person or in group Zoom calls. These kinds of responses are perfect for blue card stories where you can provide verbatim quotes, case studies or individual examples of themes revealed in numerical data.

Remember that if you are going to attribute a real person's name to a quote or reference them in a case study, you will need to show them the exact wording of the content about them and get their written permission to use it. If they don't want to be named or quoted, your alternative is to keep the essence of the content but anonymise or change the details so neither they nor anyone else could recognise them.

Open questions should be used where possible replies are unknown or too numerous to pre-code. Open questions are more demanding of respondents, but if well answered they can provide useful insight into a topic. Open questions can also be time consuming to administer and the responses difficult to analyse. Whether using open or closed questions, researchers should plan clearly how data will be analysed.

If you do decide to do some of your own research, you might get some really interesting responses and information that is different to what's already out there. More to the point, it will be *yours*. Your *unique* research findings. Your *original* book content.

THE SURPRISING CASE OF *GRANDPA ON A SKATEBOARD*

Tim Farmer, author of *Grandpa on a Skateboard: The practicalities of assessing mental capacity and unwise decision*, is a highly authoritative expert in his vitally important area of expertise: the assessment and evaluation of an individual's ability to make a decision. However, he doesn't enjoy self-promotion or even advertising his services much. The introduction of the Mental Capacity Act (2005) provided health and legal professionals with a framework to assess mental capacity, but in practice mental capacity assessments were often misunderstood and poorly conducted. Tim's was the first practical book for health and legal professionals that simplified and explained the assessment process.

Although Tim did little to promote his book when it came out (social media is not his thing), his use of real-life case studies and clear, jargon-free guidance was so brilliant at demystifying the assessment process that *Grandpa on a Skateboard* spread like wildfire through his market.

Six months after launching his book, Tim posted in an entrepreneur group asking for help: his clients had more than doubled, he had a waiting list for his services and he needed support in building out capacity and systems. The book had built his business beyond his highest expectations. Tim got help and support from the right sources and grew the structure and capacity of his business extremely effectively, and his book went on selling and promoting his services. It is now considered an industry standard as well as a core text at a number of universities and colleges across the UK.

The lesson? Don't underestimate the power your book will have to sell you and your business, and be ready for it!

YOUR AUTHOR VOICE

The style of writing can make a big difference to the positioning of your book and the impact it has on your readers, and therefore on you and your business. First-time writers are often advised to 'write how you speak.' While this idea helps ensure that your text is natural and congruent with the 'real you', if you pasted a chunk of your real-life speech into your book it would seem unfocused, long-winded, boring and would appear – strangely – unnatural. If you've ever tried to read verbatim transcripts of interviews, you'll know how hard they are to plough through. Readers don't want to see in print the ums and ers, pauses, digressions and waffling that make up everyday chat.

For some people, speaking comes more naturally than writing, and they process their thoughts through articulating them verbally. If that's you, it can make sense to 'write' your book by recording and then transcribing it, rather than writing directly.

If you are 'writing' your book by dictation – as you can in Book Magic AI – you'll get the essence of your unique voice on the page, but it's likely that you'll have to do a heavier edit on the first draft than someone who has typed their written content. Both methods are fine, but be aware that most of us speak at greater length and less precision than we write. We all have lazy habits in speech that make for difficult reading when you transfer them to the page. For example, most of us don't construct our spoken sentences efficiently to get information across in the clearest way. We can rely on our facial expressions, body language and context to add meaning to our words while talking directly to someone, but when you're engaging through written material you must do this with only words.

If you're a first-time author, you may feel tempted to adopt a writing style that you think gives you more gravitas than the way you would normally communicate. You don't need to do this. In fact, you definitely should not do this – readers want to feel personally involved with the authentic you, not lectured by some academic or business guru.

Writing that tries to be too clever comes across as self-conscious, and the reader will often feel embarrassed by the author's attempts to impress. Most people read a book first because they want the information it contains – or, more specifically, the benefits it promises – and second because they believe and trust that the author is someone who can give them that information. If what you're writing is genuine, unambiguous and easy to read, you've given the reader what they want. This is why we suggest you write to a single ideal client – your author voice will feel natural and focused to the perfect reader.

I was once given the best advice by an editor: 'Be kind to your readers.' It's in your interest for readers to enjoy reading your book and not to feel as though it's hard work to understand or an uphill battle to get through. If there's a hard way or an easy way to say something, use the easy way. If there's a long way or a short way to describe something, take the short route. Avoid technical jargon wherever possible – unless it's what your ideal client knows and feels comfortable with. Do your reader a favour by being crystal clear and not assuming they have your level of knowledge – they are reading your book precisely because they don't, so make sure your points are easy to understand. If you need to use an obscure word or an acronym, provide a definition or spell it out in full the first time you use it. If you have to use, and your readers need to learn, specialist terms, consider including a glossary at the back of the book so they can always look up anything they forget or aren't familiar with.

Check out some of the top business or self-help books in any field. Most of them use simple language and construction to tell their stories – which, when done well, is the height of sophistication.

Whatever you do, please don't try to get AI to write your book for you. AI, including the support in Book Magic AI, is brilliant at making suggestions, doing research (though always check it thoroughly – it can 'hallucinate' and make stuff up), summarising, shortening or adding length. Although it has access to more data and information than any human, and can process it more quickly than we can think, it doesn't have access to your goldmine of experience and expertise – that's in your head. However much you prompt it and show it other written work of yours, it will never be able to authentically replicate your voice. Added to this, at the moment most publishers will not accept AI-generated content from an author, and even Amazon will ask – and check – whether there is AI-generated content in your book.

THE 3TS

What I'm calling the '3Ts' is known in fiction and drama as the 'three-act structure'. Simply put, it involves ensuring that your book – and every section, chapter and subsection within it – has a clearly defined beginning–middle–end structure. This particularly applies to each chapter of a business or self-help book, though it should also be used to format shorter pieces, from articles and blog posts to emails and letters. The 3Ts are as follows:

- **T1: T**ell them what you're going to tell them. Give the big picture and/or set the scene.

- **T2: Tell them.** In the main part of your book/chapter/article/post, present all the information, adding in the necessary detail, and lead logically from one point to the next. T2 is the substantive part of your piece and may include sections with their own subheadings.
- **T3: Tell them what you've told them.** Summarise and recap; if appropriate, include a call to action. This could be a succinct paragraph, a bulleted list or a set of exercises; where appropriate, it should lead the reader into the next chapter or section.

THE WRITER PROCESS

Now we're going to get into full extraction mode. The last three steps have been loosely equivalent to the pre-extraction crushing and grinding of your ore. You can pick your analogy – dissolving in mercury or cyanide, separation in a centrifuge or magnetic separation – for setting you up for writing your first draft, but now I'll take you through the overview of the WRITER Process.

This is another place where many first-time authors lose their way. They may know who their market is, have crafted a brilliant title, written an overview and introduction and planned out their full book structure – but actually writing their book can still seem like a huge, amorphous task made up of swirling and ill-defined aspects such as drafting, checking, rewriting, reviewing, editing, proofreading… which become chaotic and overwhelming, and they can give up before they finish. They try to do too much at once, in the wrong sequence, mixing up tasks and find themselves bogged down in a chaos from which it can be difficult to emerge.

It's vital to understand that writing a book is a series of discrete tasks which, if carried out one by one and in the right order, makes it simple (if not easy!) to produce a great book to build your business. The WRITER Process, which I've honed and refined over many years, takes you through a logical and organised writing sequence that keeps you on track and moving through the necessary steps.

- **W:** Write your first draft. Your first draft doesn't have to be brilliantly written; it just has to be written. It's probably the hardest part of the entire book-writing process, even though at times it will feel exciting and exhilarating, but it has to be done. This step is about quantity – getting 30,000 to 40,000 words on the page; quality is not an issue at this point.

- **R:** Review. This is step one of your first self-edit. Don't mistake this step for proofreading or editing; reviewing is about looking at your book from the perspective of a reader rather than a writer. You might want to actually print out and read through your first draft, looking for any gaps, repetitions, inconsistencies or obvious errors, and make notes.

- **I:** Improve. This is step two of your first self-edit. With your review notes, work through your book one chapter at a time to add, remove, re-order or sharpen content. You can work on your style, too, but don't make it your main focus during this step. This is your second draft, but again, it doesn't have to be perfect yet.

- **T:** Test your second-draft manuscript with beta readers to get some early feedback. In Chapter Five, I'll tell you how to identify and brief up to six trusted colleagues, clients, authors, influencers or others who fall within the potential market of your book, to read your draft and give you honest feedback. This step is often left out, but is essential.

- **E:** Edit, based on the feedback from beta readers, to produce a final writer's draft. In this step, you get to process all the suggestions made by your beta readers and decide which to implement. Make a plan for structural or major content changes first. Then work through your document slowly, checking each sentence, as well as each paragraph, section and chapter, for sense and structure. This is your final draft.

- R: Repeat any steps you feel might be necessary, as required. You may need to revisit some of the steps, particularly four and five, until you feel your final draft is as good as you can make it. Bear in mind, though, that your manuscript will be polished and finalised by a professional editor who will pick up any mistakes you've missed.

WRITING YOUR FIRST DRAFT

The first – and, frankly, the hardest – part of writing your book is getting the initial draft out of your head and onto the page. Your first draft should be rough and ready; trying to produce a perfect manuscript first time round will waste time and distract you from shaping the basic information into a workable manuscript. Ernest Hemingway is supposed to have said, 'The first draft of anything is shit.' It's unclear whether he actually said this, but it's a good maxim and an almost mandatory assumption. Because you have such a detailed structure for your book, with every topic, case study, anecdote and piece of research listed, you can look at this step as the job of filling in the gaps – 500 words on this topic, 250 words on that case study, 1,000 words on this aspect of your model…

A good length of time to allocate for writing your first draft is about six weeks. If you let it drag on too long, it may never get finished. When you get into your writing habit (we'll learn about this shortly), you should be able to average 1,000 words an hour. If you write at this speed for one hour a day, six days a week, for six weeks, you'll have written a 36,000-word manuscript.

The Write step has three key elements, which you will need to establish for yourself; to write successfully, you will need: a schedule, a habit and discipline.

I. CREATE A WRITING SCHEDULE

Are you a lark or an owl? Do you feel most energetic, creative and focused in the early mornings, late evenings or some other time? At what point in your day can you most effectively fit your writing tasks into your schedule – and stick to them? When you work on an intensive project like writing your first draft, do you need to break it down into micro-sessions or bite-sized chunks, or stay on task for substantial periods of time?

It helps to answer these questions now because mapping out a serious writing schedule for the next six weeks is crucial to getting the job done. For many of the hundreds of authors I've mentored through writing their books, the most popular schedule has been to get up an hour earlier five or six days a week, head to the writing den, and, without getting waylaid by personal hygiene, emails, social media or anything else, get straight into writing for an hour or so, and then start the rest of their day.

One author used to set their alarm for 4am, write for two hours, return to bed at 6am and get up to begin a normal day at 8am. A bit extreme, maybe, but it worked for them. Another author used to pick two topic cards a day and would take these everywhere with them. In micro gaps in their schedule – five minutes here, ten minutes there – they would take out their cards and audio-record the next several hundred words, noting where they'd got to on the card each time. As someone who could pull focus fast and hold the place they'd got to in their head throughout the day, they got the whole book written like this in six weeks. Others prefer to nap after dinner then write late at night when the rest of the household has gone to bed. Some prefer to allocate six entire weekends to writing, and get the job done that way.

There's no right or wrong way to schedule the writing of your first draft; whatever suits you and the way your brain works best is the way to do it. If you find that your initial plans aren't as conducive to getting your first draft written as you imagined, try something different; make whatever adjustments are needed to get the job done.

Whatever schedule you decide on, make it tangible and visible in whatever you use for planning your time: online calendar, paper diary or set your schedule and get reminders in the Book Magic AI app. Physically setting out your sessions and seeing them in the context of your other events, meetings, calls and reminders will keep them in your mind and make them harder to avoid. Schedule your writing sessions as high-importance events. If you have to miss a scheduled writing session, re-schedule it ASAP and get back on track.

2. MAKE WRITING A HABIT

We all know how easy it is to get into bad habits: just do the same thing at the same time in the same way for a few days, and your morning tea break just no longer feels complete without that iced donut. Luckily, though, you can use your natural ability to form a habit to help get your first draft written.

If possible, decide on a single place where you're going to do all your writing. It might or might not be where you regularly work. Let's call it your writing den. Then, every time you go into your writing den for a writing session, bring your writing props – maybe the same mug with the same hot drink (maybe even the same iced donut) or the same music track. The more of your senses you engage as triggers, the quicker the habit will become ingrained, so also consider using a particular fragrance, wearing the same clothes...!

Sitting down to write at the same time each day may be hard at first, especially if it's early in the morning, but stick to your scheduled writing times, trying to make them as regular and similar (same place, same time, same props) as possible. Your mind will soon recognise these signs as triggers to work and switch into creative mode on cue.

You can get help with sticking to your writing habit from those around you. Tell colleagues, people at home and even clients that you are writing your first draft over the next six weeks. This way, you make yourself externally accountable for achieving your goal and can ask for support for this limited period of time. Your book, after all, will benefit your business, your family and your market.

THE DYSLEXIC AUTHOR

Mark Escott's experiences as a child and teenager were traumatic and led to him being excluded from school and finally ending up in the criminal justice system, serving a two-year suspended sentence living in a hostel for young men on probation. The likelihood of him doing anything positive with his life, let alone becoming the author of a bestselling book, seemed more than remote. Luckily for Mark, while he was living in the probation hostel, he found support and mentorship that enabled him to turn his life around.

In 2011, Mark co-founded the Life Chance Group to support young people like he had once been. It's all about innovation, pioneering a holistic approach, providing services using dedicated and expert staff, and offering proven, positive impacts to young people that allow them to feel cared for, nurtured and inspired. The aim is to allow them to reach their potential, develop confidence and be the positive members of society they were always meant to be.

During his own rehabilitation, Mark discovered that one of the reasons he had been unable to cope with education was that he was highly dyslexic. Even today, he finds the written word, reading and writing for himself, hard to process.

At the start of his Life Chance journey, Mark joined the Key Person of Influence accelerator programme and attended a day-long workshop I was giving on how to plan and write a book to build your business. Mark had come along as it was part of the programme, but didn't expect it to be useful for him. However, when I finished explaining how we were going to use coloured index cards to plan out each entrepreneur's book structure, and mentioned that we had coaches who could give extra support to people through the writing process, Mark stood up and proclaimed to the room, 'I think I can do this. I think I can write a book!' He briefly outlined his personal journey and was given a round of applause for the momentous decision he had come to.

Mark worked with one of our brilliant and sensitive Rethink Press coach/ghostwriters, speaking his book through recorded and transcribed interviews, and outsourcing the actual writing to a professional. His book, One More Life Chance, which details his journey from trauma to successful business owner and education leader, was published, became an Amazon Best Seller and is now in its second edition.

As well as telling Mark's own story, One More Life Chance also outlines the work he does with his ideal clients. It has helped to build his business and made him a high-profile influencer in his area. He is so proud of having overcome his difficulties to write the book that the story of creating it* has become a moving and popular subject in his speaking gigs.

*Any author who uses our coaching or Booksmith writing services does so in complete confidentiality. Mark gave his permission for us to tell his story.

3. DEVELOP DISCIPLINE

The first step in the WRITER Process is Write because that's all that it's about. It's not about re-reading, reviewing, researching, rewriting, editing or proofreading. You won't get your first draft of 30,000 to 40,000 words in six weeks if you do anything other than write.

When you start a writing session, don't begin by re-reading the section you wrote yesterday or checking the spelling and punctuation of an earlier piece. Don't worry about whether you've perfectly expressed your ideas or been as articulate as you'd hoped. Just get straight into today's chosen section, write it and then stop. Then, as I mentioned earlier, decide (and note down) the topic for your next session and let your subconscious go to work on it in the meantime. You'll be surprised at how much work your brain has done in the background when you start writing again.

When you're writing and you come to gaps in terms of research, statistics, contributions from others, additional case studies and so on, leave yourself a note to add these in the next step, but don't leave your manuscript to google the information you want or email someone about an interview – at least not during your writing session. If it helps, keep a running list of the additional content you will need to add to the next draft. This sort of work will be taken care of in the Review and Improve steps.

The following procrastination activities can distract you from your task of getting your first draft written and should be avoided at this stage:

- Reviewing
- Re-reading
- Formatting
- Checking quotations or facts
- Researching/googling
- Reading other books or content
- Editing
- Talking about your writing
- Worrying about writing or publishing your book
- Doom-scrolling on social media for book-related posts
- Online shopping

Because you've planned your book in such meticulous detail, you don't have to write your first draft in chronological order. If you get stuck on a topic, move on to another one that inspires you more and come back to the other one later. Working in Book Magic AI, you can click on the title of the topic or story that appeals to you, open the editor and write. At the end of your session, close it and move on with your day. Do the same every day until you've written up each one. As a bonus, this will give you a nice dopamine hit each time you complete one.

THE EMOTIONAL JOURNEY

Be aware that writing your book, especially your first draft, will be a time of emotional ups and downs. The first 5,000 words may come easily; the next 10,000 could feel much harder. At times you'll feel totally in the flow and that what you're writing is earth-shatteringly brilliant; at other times you'll curse yourself, or me, for getting you into this pointless project because everything you write has been said before and no one will want to read your book. While it's possible that the first mindset is a little overblown, the second is certainly wrong. The important thing to remember is that every author goes through these same mood swings and the only way to deal with them is to step back from your feelings and plough on through. It's not you, it's not your book – everyone on this journey will have these ups and downs. Share your feelings in the Book Magic Community group, and you'll get lots of understanding and support.

Typically, you'll experience a breakthrough at about 20,000 words: you'll come to a session and suddenly see that you're over the worst, that you've written a serious body of work that is going to be of huge value to your market and beyond and there is light at the end of the tunnel. Then you'll be on the downhill run.

There's more work to come – five more steps – but when you've completed this one, you should feel an enormous sense of satisfaction and can congratulate yourself. The hardest part is over!

SUSAN PAYTON ON WRITING

Let's follow up on Susan Payton, author of *The Business of Stories*. Susan emphasises that having a writing process to follow was helpful because, 'Left to my own devices, I wouldn't have done it that way, but it works. Trusting the process was really important – because I did that, because I stuck to it, I got my book written in three months, from start to finish.'

She went on to explain:

> 'The toughest bit of the writing was probably the messy middle. I got to a point where I felt quite overwhelmed by everything. I had notes all over the place. I had ideas. I kept thinking of more things and wondering whether I should include this or that. I can definitely see now that left to my own devices I could have got completely overwhelmed, trying to work out what to put in, what to leave out, what to keep for a later chapter, all that kind of stuff.
>
> 'So just being able to trust the process and knowing that the work at the beginning on the outline, the chapters and the detail of all the cards meant that I could keep track of what I was doing and could move cards around and see what worked better. There were steps in place, there were tools and strategies that helped me work through that messy middle bit. Even when I felt overwhelmed, I could still see where I was going with it and knew that I would get there. For people like me with a busy brain that never really switches off, having the framework and a structure to work within helped me get through the times when it all felt like a lot.'

FIVE
REFINING

FIRE AND ACID

If you've followed my advice and written your first draft without stopping, reviewing, tweaking, editing or researching, it will be rough and ready – as it should be. You've worked hard at extracting the gold of your IP from the ore of your broader experience and expertise. Your first draft is like raw gold. The next steps of the WRITER Process are all about refining your gold into its purest form.

The differences in value between raw and refined gold are substantial. Raw gold, though valuable, is less sought-after due to its impurities and the additional refining costs it incurs. Market demand for refined gold is significantly higher, driving up its price. This is also the case for the IP in a well-written and produced book as opposed to lower quality content and production.

There are a few different methods of refining gold but, depending upon the quantity of gold you are working with and the desired level of purity, the two most common are the use of high-temperature flame or chemicals.

Refining metals with flame is one of the oldest methods on record. Mentioned even in the Bible, refining by fire is the preferred method for larger quantities of gold. In ancient times, this process involved a craftsman sitting next to a hot fire with molten gold in a crucible, stirring and skimming it to remove the impurities or dross that rose to the top of the molten metal. With flames reaching temperatures in excess of 1,000 degrees Celsius, the job of a gold refiner was a dangerous occupation. The tradition remains largely untouched today with the exception of a few advancements in safety and precision.

The second method of refining gold involves the use of nitric and hydrochloric acids to dissolve the impurities in the gold ore; these are then neutralised and washed away, taking the impurities with them. The resulting product is a muddy substance that is almost pure gold (99.999% or 24K). This is dried until it is a powdered residue and then heated with a torch or other heat source to melt the gold powder into useable gold.

You can pick which refining analogy works better for you in taking your first draft through the next stages – or apply fire to some and chemicals to others. Maybe your work through Reviewing, Improving and Editing might seem a bit like dissolving the impurities of your writing in acid, while Testing your second draft with beta readers might feel more like applying fire!

REVIEW

In step two of the WRITER Process, it is important that you start by taking a break from your manuscript. Give yourself a day or two away from your first draft and try not to even think about it, let alone look at it. Then, print it out. If you're using Book Magic AI, export your manuscript to a Word document and print a hard copy.

This is a vital, distinct step in the WRITER Process, and one that is often left out or mixed up with proofing and editing. When you take the time to carry out this task on its own before moving on to the next steps, you bring extra clarity to your manuscript, which will show up in the final draft.

The first stage of Review is to get some separation from your book. The important thing with editing is the ability to take a step back. It's time to be more objective about what you've written because the symbiotic relationship between you, what you see on the screen and what you type with your fingers on the keyboard is part of you. It's in your head and it's hard to be objective about it. However, when you print out your manuscript, it becomes a different, separate thing.

Once it's printed out, you need to swap your writing habit for a reading habit. The next part of the Review step will consist of you making notes throughout your manuscript. Of course you can mark it up in an online document if you prefer. At this point you are not looking to perfect the spelling, punctuation, grammar or even style. What you're looking for here in the first instance is overall structural integrity and flow. Is the book taking you as a reader on a step-by-step journey where everything is coming in the right order? Do you learn one thing and then move on to the next?

You're also looking for consistency. Consistency is the hallmark of a book that reads professionally – that feels like it's been written by a professional writer. Each chapter should have a consistent structure: an Introduction and a Conclusion, and in between a similar amount of subsection headings, case studies, stories from your own journey and supporting data. It really does matter that your chapters are all consistently similar lengths.

Work through your whole book, slowly and carefully, with a pen in hand. As you go through, make notes about what needs adding, what needs cutting and where there's been repetition. As you read, check:

- That the overall structure makes sense and is consistent.
- That everything flows logically – is your framework or model working?
- Are your chapters and sections roughly the same length?
- Have you introduced and summarised each chapter?
- Do you have enough case studies, anecdotes and other stories?
- What other research do you need to do?

- What needs cutting?
- What needs adding or expanding on?

By the time you've reviewed the full manuscript, it should be covered in notes. Once you have done this, your Review is complete and you are ready to move on to the next step.

IMPROVE

Because you have such detailed notes from your Review, the Improve step will be simple. You'll know what you need to do, add or change to improve your manuscript, and can get from first to second draft quickly.

Switch back into writer mode and return to your manuscript with your paper notes by your side. Tackle the biggest issues that your Review has highlighted first. If you've found problems with the structure of your book, deal with them as your first improvement. This is particularly key if an overhaul of the objective or message of the book is in order. Don't be disheartened by the prospect of substantial reworking; even if you need to take some processing time before getting down to it, the solution will become clear. If you address structural issues at this stage rather than later in the WRITER Process, your book will be better for it.

You might have decided that a whole chapter is in the wrong place and needs moving, or that sections within one or more of the chapters should be re-ordered. This is super-simple with the Plan function in Book Magic AI – just drag and drop. If you move chapters or sections, though, remember to check for all other references to this content throughout the rest of the book, and review the chapter or section holistically again when you have finished.

When you've done your best to fix your big-picture issues, work through the manuscript from start to finish, correcting every point you've noted from your Review and anything else that shows up as you progress. This will include the task of sorting out the smaller concerns of filling gaps in content, carrying out additional research, trimming material or sharpening up the presentation of your ideas, which will clarify the content in your own mind as well as in those of your readers.

Your Review may have shown you that your authorial voice wasn't quite how you want to come across to your readers. Were there places where you became overly technical, when you are writing for a non-professional market? Or, did you over-explain in a way that might seem patronising to a readership well versed in your area of expertise?

Although this isn't your final edit, try to improve any areas where your author voice didn't feel right. You may not have got into your writing stride until two or three chapters in, so check that your early chapters have the same feel as the later ones – the feel of you comfortably talking to your ideal client.

Keep an eye out for consistency as you improve the second draft of your manuscript. Ensure that your chapters are all a similar (but not necessarily identical) length, that the sections within each chapter are similarly divided up and that the chapters are all structured in the same way. Each chapter should start with some kind of introduction and end with a conclusion. These could be short paragraphs, bullet points or, for the conclusion, a short exercise or checklist that shows the reader what they've learned.

At the end of the Improve step, you will have created a far superior second draft, making it (and you) ready for the next step: Test.

THE MARKETING AGENCY BOOK

Matt Elwell is the co-founder and director of Elite Closing Academy, an agency that trains people to bring in more sales revenue by improving their confidence, their mindset and, in particular, their communication skills. They deliver this in a number of ways – live events, mentorship and certified training programmes.

Matt initially wrote his first book, *Open with a Close: The twelve point guide to closing more sales*, because he wanted to share his message that 'there is a modern way of communicating aligned with personal values, focused around interaction and great communication skills.'

Matt says they now use the book to 'create awareness, for entrepreneurs and business owners in the industry, that there is a [sales] solution out there that is all about great communication and interaction.' Among numerous competitors offering similar services, Matt's agency has a strong brand, based in avoiding 'hard tactics' in favour of personal values and communication skills. Showcasing that brand through the book helps them stand out in a crowded market, differentiating them from the competition, and also means readers understand what they'll get when they hire the agency.

Matt's first book was so successful, and he has so much business gold to mine, that he wrote a second, *Cold to Sold: Serve, sell & scale your way to business success*, which was published in August 2024, and says 'writing books has been a big part of the journey' to his own success.

TEST

Having written a second draft of your manuscript in the Improve step, you are now going to Test your book on a select readership – your beta readers. You've written a first draft, stood back from your manuscript to review it and then improved your book as much as you can for the moment. Now the most important thing you can do is ask a few trusted individuals to give you their honest opinions. This, by the way, is not a task you should be employing professionals for; nor should you be offering payment to anyone.

Unsurprisingly, most people find this quite scary, which is why I suggested that this step is like refining gold with fire. Scary as it may feel, this process is crucial to refining your book into pure gold. Every author I've worked with, without exception, has found that it's an incredibly positive experience, that they get lots of affirmation and positive feedback from the people they've chosen, far more than they thought they would. However, where you do get suggestions about how to improve your manuscript, that constructive feedback is full of insight and really helps you get to a great final draft. This is the gold dust that you're looking for. Yes, sometimes it means that you have to do a bit more work to get your last pass to where it should be, but that's fine – getting the best possible end result is what we're interested in.

CHOOSING YOUR BETA READERS

You want to ask no more than six beta readers to read your second draft. Two of these should be people who are your peers. They might be colleagues. They might be partners you work with. They might be people in your industry – not direct competitors of course, but experts who have the same information and experience that you do, so they can critique your book from a knowledge level equal to your own.

Then pick two more beta readers who represent your ideal clients. They could be past or perhaps even current clients. You could ask a prospect who you want to attract. These two people will be able to tell you whether you have pitched your book right, whether you're talking to them in a way that would attract them to come and hire you.

Those first four beta readers are the most important. However, it's also useful to get feedback from a non-specialist, someone who's not necessarily in your market at all. This could perhaps be an intelligent business book reader, or someone just interested in business, who can look at your book, read it and see if it engages them, even if they're not a potential client or even especially interested in your subject area. You can ask them: Is it readable? Is it interesting? Do they enjoy the journey it takes them on?

A final, really useful person to recruit as a beta reader, if you can find them, is a key person in your industry – who could also potentially be the person to write your Foreword. You might know them, in which case approaching them is easy. If you don't know them, you could make contact on social media by liking and commenting on their posts for a bit. Then go for a more personal approach – DM or email – and ask them if they'd consider being a beta reader for your book. Send them your Introduction as a standalone document (this is one reason why it's so helpful to write it upfront) to show them what your book is about. If they say no, or ignore your request, move on. There are other people out there.

You need a minimum of two beta readers and six is the maximum. Don't use more than six because the feedback becomes overwhelming and confusing, so choose these people carefully. You might worry that you're asking all these people a huge favour, but most people are flattered to be asked to give feedback on an author's manuscript. The worst they can do is say no, and if they won't or can't do it, then they're not the right person to help you at this time.

BRIEFING YOUR BETA READERS

Ask your beta readers how they would like to read your manuscript – as an invited collaborator in the Book Magic AI app where they can leave comments; via a Word document where they can also leave comments and make inline suggestions; or even in hard copy. If it's the latter, supply your beta readers with a tidy, printed copy of your manuscript and ask them to read it with a pen in hand. Some will prefer it loose leaf; for others it's worth getting a bound copy if it makes the task easier for them.

Be clear with your beta readers about what sort of feedback you want from them: it must be honest, specific and constructive, including positive reactions as well as improvements they think you could make. Make sure they know that this is a draft, unedited manuscript, and that you do not want them to correct your spelling, punctuation or grammar as that will be done later by a professional editor.

Ask them to tell you:

- What they thought the book was going to teach them and whether it lived up to their expectations
- Their overall reaction – and especially whether they wanted to read on to find out what you were going to say next
- Whether they were entirely clear about what you were telling them all the time; ask them to mark sections where they felt lost or confused and to explain why
- Whether they found it easy to read and understand (bearing in mind that this is only your second draft)
- Where they got bored, felt you were going on too long or found that you were repeating yourself
- Whether there were any obvious gaps or inconsistencies
- What they enjoyed most
- What they would most suggest that you change

You'll need to give your beta readers a deadline for reviewing your manuscript. Two weeks should be long enough if you give them notice, clear instructions and provide the manuscript in the format they're most comfortable with. For best results, contact your beta readers well in advance and give them as accurate timings as possible for when you will deliver the manuscript and the deadline for receiving their feedback. Make sure they've booked this job into their schedule and won't try to put it off at the last minute.

Remember to tell them that you'll thank them individually, in print, in your Acknowledgements, and will send them a personal signed copy when the book is published.

When your beta readers have given you their feedback, you will have the information you need to carry out the next step, Edit.

EDIT

When you get the feedback from your beta readers, enjoy the positives, but accept any negative responses from honest readers at this stage as a gift; they may save you from rejection from publishers, a poor reception from your prospects or bad reviews from your critics or paying readers.

Only at this point, with all the notes and critiques from your beta readers, will you have an idea of the size and complexity of your editing task. Whether your structure hangs together but your style and grammar need another look, or whether you realise that an overhaul of some sections is required, don't be daunted.

First, collate all your feedback. This is easy in Book Magic AI. It might not all be consistent: your readers may disagree with each other and take different points of view. Take seriously anything that two or more readers agree on. Try to assess criticism objectively, even though you would rather listen to the praise. Decide which suggestions you are going to accept and implement – in the end, this is your book, and you're under no obligation to do what your beta readers suggest.

BE SYSTEMATIC

It is crucial to be systematic when editing. You must stop thinking like a writer and try to take on the mindset of a professional editor. This means stepping back from your book and looking for what might be missing, such as a crucial step, a case study or a key piece of information in the right place. Is there too much personal opinion or too much focus on your own experience? Or too little of you personally in the book? Are the quotes and case studies furthering your message or getting in the way? Be systematic – and ruthless.

BIG PICTURE, THEN THE DETAIL

As with previous steps in the WRITER Process, work from the wider structural issues first, through the chapter-by-chapter changes and then, once you have resolved any big issues, go through the manuscript a second time and edit for fine detail.

Finally, check your facts – dates, science, events, numbers, people's names and quotations (which must be accurate and referenced). Your professional editor will come back to you for anything they find missing or wrong, but it helps them and you to get this right first time.

REPEAT

While you should take your time with the self-editing process before handing your manuscript to your publisher or editor, it's important that you do eventually let go. It's easy to feel there's always more you can do to improve your final manuscript, but most authors get to the point where they can't see the wood for the trees and yet more tweaking doesn't improve anything. You'll be amazed when you get your copy-edited manuscript back how an objective professional can give the final polish to all your hard work. For this reason, Repeat is the final, optional step of the WRITER Process for getting your book written and self-edited to a high standard. So far you have written, reviewed, improved, tested and edited your manuscript – at which point it may seem as though you have done enough. Whether or not you use this last step depends on whether you feel the need to go through the last two steps again to bring your book even closer to perfection.

Having given your book a final self-edit and incorporated the feedback you've chosen to implement from your beta readers, some authors find it useful to ask one or more of their beta readers to give the manuscript another pass. Especially if they suggested and you have implemented any quite substantial changes.

Or, at this stage, you may have initially submitted your manuscript to your publisher and they've asked you to make a few more changes before it's ready to go into their production process, which will usually start with a copy-edit.

THE FOREWORD

Often misunderstood, and sometimes misspelled (as 'forward' or 'foreward'), a Foreword is a useful – though not essential – part of your book. It sets the stage for you, the author, and, if written by someone with a well-known or often-searched name, it can boost marketing and sales of your book.

The Foreword lets the reader know, in a short summary, what the book is about and why it is significant. It can contextualise and sell the book (and the author) from an objective but knowledgeable point of view.

WHO WRITES THE FOREWORD?

Not you! You write your own Introduction, but the Foreword writer should be an experienced and qualified person in your or a related industry or market, or simply someone well known whose name will validate the work and endorse the expertise of you as the author. It could be someone you asked to be a beta reader who gave you good feedback – in which case, you can ask them to make that the basis of their Foreword.

WHAT SHOULD THEY SAY?

Some Forewords are short, as little as 200 words, but 500 to 1,000 words is ideal. The writer of the Foreword should think in terms of engaging the reader quickly. It should start with an intriguing hook – a question or statement that grabs attention and introduces the subject matter.

Then, in a few more paragraphs, the Foreword should:

- Set the context in which the Foreword writer knows about the market and its problems, and establish a personal/professional connection to the subject of the book. It's a good place for the writer to subtly blow their own trumpet; it's one of the payoffs for writing a Foreword for someone else's book, making it a win-win for both of you.

- Summarise the market's (readers') central problem or question (the reason why they picked up or bought the book) and the author's big promise (their solution to the problem/question, as provided in the book).

- Explain how the Foreword writer knows the author and their expertise in this field. It should emphasise how well the author does what they do (outside the book, in their business) and, therefore, how qualified the author is to write this book.

- Highlight some specific content, areas or solutions in the book as a 'teaser' to the reader, and talk about specific benefits the book will bring to the reader.

- End with a big plug for the book and its author, and sign off with the Foreword writer's name, credentials or title/company, the title of a recent book (if they have written one) and perhaps their website URL.

SUSAN PAYTON AND HER BETA READERS

Susan Payton, who you by now know well, author of *The Business of Stories*, was shocked when she got to the Test step in the WRITER Process:

> 'When you told me to send my second draft to my advance readers, I was like, "What? It's not ready! It's nowhere near ready. Surely, I should get it to the point where I think it's finished and then get feedback?" But no, your advice was to send it at this point in the process. I'm so glad I did because the feedback was brilliant!
>
> 'I also followed your advice about how to choose my advance readers. I chose people that I knew would give me really good, constructive feedback, which is what I wanted. I sent it to six, and five of them read the manuscript and sent their responses back to me, which was a great result. The feedback was incredibly useful, it really helped me to make the book flow much better. You get a bit blind with it all when you've written it and read it however many times; just having an outside view at that point in the process was so helpful.
>
> 'I got all the feedback in, I read it and processed it. Some of it I ignored; some of it I thought was brilliant. I made the edits I wanted to make, taking the feedback on board, and then took myself off to a coffee shop and read it as if I was a reader. Then I came back, did a few more edits, and that was it.
>
> 'I sent it off to Rethink Press and my wonderful editor polished it up, ready for publication.'

SIX
THE GOLDEN KEY

CREATING GOLD BARS

Through prospecting, mining, extracting and refining the content of your goldmine, you have a book-shaped manuscript. This now has to go into the final phase of creating the gold bar – a professionally published book – that you can take out into the world to share your value and trade it for its true worth.

You have three options for publishing your book: traditional, DIY (or 'self') and hybrid publishing. In this chapter we'll review what those options entail, and the pros and cons of each one, so that you can make a decision on which is best for you.

Up until about twenty years ago and the emergence of print-on-demand (POD) and online book retailers, there was only one credible route to getting a book published: a contract with what we now call a 'traditional' publishing house. We call them 'traditional' not because they publish a particular type of book, or have an old-fashioned way of working; it's their business model that is traditional. These publishers, either the massive global businesses or the specialist independents, all invest in the creation and distribution of the book and then have a single means of getting a return on that investment: selling individual copies of books either to the public or to the author.

Traditional publishers used to be the gatekeepers to distribution channels and the (traditionally) only retail outlets: bookstores. 'Vanity publishers', as they were then derisively called, could create and print your book, for a fee, but they couldn't access the wholesale and retail chain to sell books to customers. Happily, there is no longer any such barrier to getting your book in print and selling via the same channels as the traditional publishers. With the barriers down, though, authors need to make informed choices about which route will best suit their needs, and there are positives and negatives to all of them.

TRADITIONAL PUBLISHING

Traditional publishers include the big-name, international publishers that everyone has heard of, often known as the 'Big Five' (depending on who has taken over whom lately). Each one owns a range of imprints devoted to different types of fiction and non-fiction, including business and self-help books. There is also a wide range of smaller, independent traditional publishers, several with their own niches in non-fiction and business or self-help publishing.

In the traditional publishing business model, the publisher contracts the author to publish their book. The contract may include the publisher buying the copyright of the author's IP for a defined period of time, which could limit the author's freedom to use their material for other purposes. The publisher might – though this is a diminishing practice – pay the author an 'advance': money in advance of publication that will be recouped by the publisher from the author's royalties from sales. Many authors never actually recoup their advance and begin receiving royalties themselves – in other words, the only money they ever see is the advance, which, unless they are a famous author or celebrity, when calculated as an hourly rate of payment for their work, is probably under minimum wage. Paying advances that are not recouped is a financial drain for traditional publishers, so increasingly only big-name authors are receiving them.

A big traditional publisher is likely to pay an author 8% to 10% of net receipts from sales of their book (after production, printing and distribution costs, and less the discount payable to wholesalers and retailers); this can work out to be as little as 20p from the sale of an average-priced book. Smaller publishers, especially those who only use POD distribution (more on this shortly), may pay a higher royalty rate.

The traditional publisher then takes all the financial responsibility for getting the book published, usually including editing, design, typeset, cover design and printing. Traditional publishers, as well as publishing through online retailers like Amazon, will typically produce an 'upfront' print run of the book (usually between 500 and 3,000 copies – or more if you're an established author with a sales track record) from an offset litho printer and distribute it through physical bookstores. This, however, is becoming increasingly expensive and is often only profitable for well-known authors or other bestsellers where publishers can invest in in-store merchandising (either paid for directly or by offering a discount). The bigger publishers use their high-selling books to subsidise the distribution of new authors, but smaller traditional publishers may choose not to risk funding the print and distribution costs of an untried author's book.

Distributing a book through online retailers is often done through POD. This is a digital printing process through which small print runs (as low as one copy at a time) can be produced at a reasonable price, as they are ordered by purchasers. While the quality of POD books can be slightly lower than offset litho (traditional) printed books, POD technology and costs are improving all the time. POD allows publishers to avoid the need to invest money printing books in advance of sales and cuts down the risk of having unsold stock returned or pulped.

Leaving aside the cost of print, storage and shipping, selling books through physical bookstores is scarcely profitable for publishers, and therefore authors, because retailers often insist on stocking titles on a 'sale or return' basis. Any unsold books will not be paid for and must be returned to the publisher at their own expense, or simply destroyed. Mainstream publishers typically give a book three months in bookstores before giving up hope of making further sales. If the book doesn't perform well, they abandon the marketing and distribution to focus on new titles, and the author's book is sold for pennies (often less than the cost to produce it) or destroyed.

Traditional publishing is most effective for authors who are already well known in their fields, have a big following and a broad market subject, and will benefit from the kudos of being associated with a specific publishing company. Although landing a big-name publishing contract is the dream for many aspiring authors, being published with a mainstream traditional publisher is not always ideal for entrepreneur authors.

THE PROS OF TRADITIONAL PUBLISHING

Kudos: For many authors, the cachet of being taken on by a well-known publishing house is key to their strategy, and the backing of such a publisher can translate into a higher media profile, higher fees and a better shot at fame.

Distribution: Your book (at least for a limited time) is more likely to find its way onto bookstores' shelves than it would be using other publishing options. Although being on a shelf in a bookshop among loads of other books is no guarantee of success (especially as more sales are happening online), it is likely you will make more actual sales (though not necessarily more profit).

Marketing: All big, and some small, traditional publishers have in-house marketing and publicity departments to support authors. They can get great PR coverage for the right book, but all publishers, even the biggest, will only contract a book by an author with a big social media following, who gives talks and workshops where books can be sold and who has a good marketing plan for their book. They will still require the author to work hard to promote themselves and their book to generate maximum sales. Traditional publishers look for authors who sell books.

Focus: A traditional publisher takes on the project management of getting your book published, allowing you to concentrate on the main job of writing your next one.

Risk aversion: If you're risk averse or don't have money to spare, a traditional publishing contract with a traditional publisher means you won't have to spend any money on the production of your book – and if you're lucky or famous, they may even give you an advance. However, given the level of competition for these contracts, many authors choose to pay for a professional edit before submitting their manuscript to an agent or publisher.

THE CONS OF TRADITIONAL PUBLISHING

Loss of freedom: When you work for a publisher (because that's what your contract will mean), some of your creative freedom and freedom of speech will be lost. The publisher will need to ensure your book fits their brand and they'll have their own (often good, though sometimes not) ideas about how the book should look, what it should be called, what it should be about and how it should be positioned. Many contracts will also include a clause saying how long you've got to complete your manuscript. Failing to meet the deadlines imposed by your publisher can result in you losing your contract and your advance.

Loss of control: A traditional publisher may limit what you can do with your book, your use of the book content in other media, such as a course or workshop, or even what you can say about your book. You might need to get approval for a marketing or advertising campaign you'd like to run, and your ability to write another book with another publisher (or even to self-publish) could be subject to certain conditions in your contract. You may think you're only committing to one book, but you could end up signing over your future work too.

Loss of ownership: Many large publishers will stipulate that they own the rights to your work in other languages, territories and formats. Be careful what you're signing and ensure you know your rights. You could end up watching your publisher get rich while you remain unrewarded.

Lack of marketing: The average mainstream publisher organises distribution, lists your book in their catalogue and puts out a press release. These days, as an author, and whichever way you publish your book, marketing and promotion is 100% your job. Even if you're a big-name celebrity or your last book was a bestseller (which you will have had to work hard to promote), your publisher still won't be able to do the interviews or manage your social media for you. You have to be the spokesperson for your book, and that means you need to hustle and be adept at social media. Even so, you may find that your publisher, in the interest of protecting their reputation, will ask you to run your own marketing plans by them first.

Loss of profit: As the publisher has taken on all the financial risk to get your book published, you will be paid the 'mouse's share' of the proceeds from your book sales. If you have used an agent (often the only way to get your book in front of a big publisher), you will have to give 10% to 15% of your income to them. In fact, the publisher will pay your agent, who will then pay you – after they've taken their fee. Trying to land a good agent can be just as difficult as landing a publishing deal. The need for an agent adds an extra layer of time, control and cost to your publication journey.

Loss of time and opportunity: Until you start selling books, the whole process is still a 'cost-money' exercise; you could spend more money and time chasing a publishing contract or agent than if you'd just self-published. In that time, who knows how many opportunities you may have missed?

Lack of speed: Publishing behemoths are full of talented people, but the organisations themselves are slow, cumbersome and full of political, financial and shareholder pressures. This all leads to a long delay between landing a deal and selling any books. In addition to the time spent courting and signing with a traditional publisher, it typically takes at least a year from delivering your manuscript for your book to be out and selling.

Expensive author copies: The traditional publishers' business model is based on exploiting the IP published in your book, so their aim is to maximise profit on books sold. This also applies to author copies. If you're an entrepreneurial author and are planning to give books away to build a list or sell direct at events and seminars, expect traditional publishers to offer you only a small discount on your author copies, even if you're ordering thousands. Traditional publishers publish books to build their business; not yours.

DIY/SELF-PUBLISHING

Authors have been self-publishing books for hundreds of years, but the advent of digital printing, POD and online self-publishing platforms in the twenty-first century now enable any author who chooses to publish their own book to directly access the same market as traditional publishers. Many self-publishing authors take this route not as a last resort, but because they can make more income per retail sale than a traditional publisher will allow them to, and because managing the whole publishing process themselves is a cheaper and more hands-on option than hybrid publishing.

DIY publishing can look like an attractive publishing option financially, but it involves an author becoming a micro publisher – and the business of publishing, from production of a good book to getting it distributed worldwide, is much more complex than it might appear. If you are not technically knowledgeable, prepared to put in a lot of time learning how to do it properly or are reluctant to pay other professionals to help you publish, you will need to think carefully about whether this option can work for you.

'Self-publishing' is in fact a misnomer. No single individual can carry out all the functions that are required for a book to read, look and feel professional, and to get full distribution through the complicated systems and databases that make up the global book distribution system. You can make this process as cheap and easy as possible by taking your book through to self-publishing in the Book Magic AI app.

Self-publishing is effective for fiction or serial authors whose books are their products (rather than sales tools for their businesses), who prefer to keep control of their own publishing process and for whom learning the intricacies of the publishing industry is worthwhile.

THE PROS OF SELF-PUBLISHING

Freedom, control and ownership: Your book is your own, and no publisher can tell you what they want in it, how it should look and where it should be positioned. You can do whatever you like with your own material: write it as you want it to appear, repackage it in different formats, give some away free…

Maximum profit: As all the financial risk in getting your book published has been yours, and the work in getting it distributed has been yours, so 100% of your profit from sales comes directly to you.

Time and opportunity: You are working to your own timescales – on the one hand, you have no deadlines, unless you set them yourself; on the other, you are not waiting on other people's input and schedules. You can take as long or as short a time as you like to write, get the other aspects of publishing sorted out and spend as much or as little time as you want on marketing and promotion.

Low risk: You can spend comparatively little, if you so choose, on professional editing, cover design, interior design and typesetting, proofreading, e-book conversion, setting up your distribution and printing your own copies. If you have time to spend learning the publishing ropes that wouldn't be better spent making money in your own area of expertise, you have nothing to lose in doing this.

Easy to do: With Book Magic AI, you can get your book AI-proofed, ensuring the grammar, punctuation and spelling are correct, have your cover and interior designed within the app and get your book published on Amazon KDP. However, I still suggest that you insert a human copy-editor into the process, at the very least.

THE CONS OF SELF-PUBLISHING

Lower kudos or reputational damage: In some areas there is still lower status associated with a self-published book, especially if your book appears amateurish in its content or production values. The problem with self-publishing is that unless you have done it multiple times, you don't know what you don't know and your book may have some substandard elements. If your book is badly written or edited you could be doing your reputation more harm than good by having your book out there.

Distribution: You will not be able to get as comprehensive a listing with the databases, printers and wholesalers who service online and physical bookstores if you are not a professional publisher with a list of at least ten books and additional subscriptions to their services.

Project management: Unless you pay someone else to manage the process for you, every aspect of the publication of your book is down to you. To be sure of a professional result, it is safest to find and engage professional human specialists like editors and designers. You then need to manage and coordinate their input to be sure that they have done the job required to the right standard, and also learn the technical side of book production, publishing, distribution and marketing.

Lack of marketing: Even more than with other kinds of publisher, as a self-published author marketing and promotion is 110% your job. You have to be the social marketer, PR agent and spokesperson for your book, and that means hustling. Book Magic AI can help with this by creating marketing copy and managing social media posting.

Post-publication hassle: Deciding to self-publish means you're taking the decision to become a publisher. You will have no one to support you with marketing, printing or the business side of things after your book has been published. This can involve hassles like invoicing, chasing payment, sending books for legal deposit (a legal requirement in the UK and other countries), shipping to distributors or customers, collating royalty information for tax purposes and much more.

HYBRID PUBLISHING

Over the years, there have been several terms for the kind of publishing that offers a bridge between traditional and self-publishing, including supported publishing, paid-for publishing, cohort publishing, self-publishing companies or partnership publishing. Some of these are actually hybrid publishers; others are what I would call assisted self-publishing businesses – they help an author go through the production process until they ultimately self-publish their book.

A true hybrid publisher is a publishing business that operates in the same way as a traditional publishing business, but with a different business model – usually that the author pays for a publishing package that covers the cost of the production of their book from submission of manuscript to the book being for sale online and they have physical copies in their hand. Either the author or the publisher owns the book's ISBN and is therefore 'the publisher' of the book. If the publisher owns it, they have published the book and the author has not self-published. If the author owns the ISBN, they are the publisher and the company that has provided their publishing services is just that – a publishing services company – and not their 'publisher'.

The business book publishing industry and its authors, especially in the UK, have now converged on the term 'hybrid publishing' to describe a publishing contract where the author pays a professional publishing company for the costs associated with producing their book – such as editing, design and typesetting, proofreading, cover design, ISBN, e-book conversion, uploading to printers, wholesale and retail distribution, royalty collection/calculation and ongoing trouble-shooting – and the publisher pays the author a more generous royalty than they would receive from a traditional publisher.

This is what we've been doing at Rethink Press since 2011.

Our many authors, and those who have published with other hybrid publishers, choose not to jump through the hoops of chasing a traditional publishing contract, with the uncertainty of ever gaining a contract and the inevitable delays even if they did. They choose not to spend time learning the technicalities of publishing for themselves, nor sourcing and managing the range of individual professionals whose input they would need to self-publish. They want their books published professionally in a short timeframe to underpin their platform of niche expertise, and they want to work with publishing industry experts, enabling them to focus on developing their core business during the publishing process and then transforming that business with the excellent book that they end up with.

In some writing and publishing circles (more usually fiction), the concept of paid-for publishing is still a little tarred with the brush of the legacy practice of 'vanity publishing'. Before the advent of POD and online booksellers, anyone who wanted to publish their own book had to do it using so-called vanity publishers. These companies made a portion of their money by persuading hapless authors, often of autobiographies and personal memoirs, as well as novels and information books, to pay for big print runs of their book. The authors would then have to store many copies (sometimes thousands) of these volumes, with no means of distributing them other than gifts/sales to family and friends, or paid advertising. Unsurprisingly, vanity publishers earned themselves a bad name (literally) and a bad reputation. Traditional publishers and traditionally published authors looked down on these kinds of self-published authors as not having written a good enough book to be accepted by a 'real' publisher.

With self-published books, in print and e-book format, now selling as well as traditionally published books, this is (mostly) no longer the case. The Business Book Awards has helped to create a level playing field in the perceptions of different routes to publishing by accepting and encouraging submissions from every kind of publisher, and the knowledgeable and diverse judging panel has picked winners who have published through a range of means.

Reputable hybrid publishing companies should be entirely transparent about their costs and contracts and provide authors with only the services they need and want. There are some 'self-publishing companies', both large and small, that continue the ethos of the original vanity publishers: make money at all costs, especially at the author's cost, in every possible way. This can involve providing poor services at high cost, over-selling and under-performing, selling services such as marketing and promotion as certain ways to sell books when such claims are rarely justified, and outsourcing the services to minimally qualified (and probably poorly remunerated) 'associates'. Most Big Five traditional publishers, having realised the value of the paid-for publishing business model, have an associated hybrid publishing business – but don't be fooled into thinking that if you publish with one of these, the traditional publisher will look more favourably on your next book. It doesn't happen.

As an author, you should always check out hybrid publishers before working with them. Try to find at least one author who has worked with the company and see what their experience was like, if it hasn't been recommended to you by one. If a hybrid publisher, or self-publishing company, tries to upsell you anything you didn't ask, plan, want, need or budget for, look elsewhere.

Similarly, check the contract you are offered by a hybrid publisher with great care. At Rethink Press, our contracts are for the exclusive right to publish your work in print, e-book and audiobook format in all territories for five years – a typical length of time for any publisher. We do not take control of your IP or restrict your ability to use your own material in other ways. If you wanted to end the contract early for a good reason, we would consider releasing you from it, believing that an unhappy author or negative relationship means it's not working for either party. Some authors who have published with big 'self-publishing' companies have found themselves unable to get released from contracts they thought they had flexibility with. The Business Book ROI study highlighted how this increased flexibility led to higher satisfaction among authors:

> 'While more than 70% of traditionally published and hybrid-published authors agreed that they were satisfied with their publishers, hybrid-published authors were twice as likely to volunteer strong agreement. Authors, especially experienced authors, agreed that they used an efficient process that aligned with both their personal career strategy and their business strategy.'
> *A Comprehensive Study of Business Book ROI* report by Amplify Publishing Group, Gotham Ghostwriters, and Thought Leadership Leverage, 2024

PROS OF HYBRID PUBLISHING

Freedom, control and ownership: Your book is your own, and a reputable hybrid publisher will work with you to make your book exactly how you want and need it to be, in content, design and positioning. All professional hybrid publishers will tell you exactly what the cost of your publishing package is before starting work, and they will allow you to pay in reasonable instalments. This is much harder to do if you're managing your own team of freelancers/suppliers.

Professional production: The editor, designers and typesetter will be experienced in the business book genre, used to working with authors such as you and with each other. You will not have to source the professional contributors to your book, and with their input your book will have a thorough edit and proofread, and a professional look and feel.

Project management: As well as not having to search for the right specialists to create your book, the time-consuming and intensive task of managing them will be done by an experienced publishing professional, leaving you free to start marketing, working on your core business, and/or writing your next book. They will also manage your royalties and deal with queries and issues post-publication.

A 'real' publisher: Although there is decreasing stigma about self-publishing, your book will have all the benefits of being produced and branded by a professional publishing company. Like a traditional publisher, hybrid publishers have existing accounts with wholesalers, retailers, distribution databases and printers, so your book will have better distribution than a self-published book and your publisher will be able to access cheaper print rates than any individual author can. They should also be proactive in selling the foreign rights of your book to overseas publishers, attending the London and Frankfurt Book Fairs to promote their catalogue as widely as possible. Some hybrid publishers of business books are well known and as aspirational as independent traditional publishers.

Quality: If you choose well, the end product will be high quality and professional. The edit, typeset, design and quality of your content should be top-notch, and a hybrid publisher will offer their professional advice and expertise while working to make your book what you need it to be for your brand and business.

High royalties: As you have taken a lot of the upfront risk of publishing your book, your hybrid publisher should be paying you higher royalties. At Rethink Press, we pay authors a royalty rate of 60% of net income on retail sales.

Easy access to stock: A good hybrid publisher will be transparent about costs, should you wish to order author copies to sell direct. Because they're likely using a variety of POD and offset litho printers, it's possible to order small or large quantities at a decent price. In the case of Rethink Press, we pass on the print savings directly to our authors and keep pricing transparent.

THE HEALTH AND FITNESS BOOK

Many leaders in the health and fitness industry have found having a book to their name gets their unique ideas out there, and helps them reach more clients and generate repeat business. One such leader is Brian Keane, owner of Brian Keane Fitness and host of The Brian Keane Podcast, one of the top health podcasts on Apple Podcasts.

Brian wrote and released his first book, *The Fitness Mindset*, in 2017. He says it has grown his business in so many ways, one being that he has had a large number of clients sign up to his paid programme after having read his book. In fact, Brian has two bestselling books that have helped him reach his business goals, and rise to many of the challenges of a health and fitness business.

Many small business leaders in the health and fitness niche struggle with fluctuations in client activity and revenue throughout the year, such as during holidays or summer. A book can bridge the gap for potential clients who want to develop or reach their fitness goals but can't commit right now due to budget or time constraints.

Brian's books are an excellent way to keep clients engaged and committed to their fitness programmes over the long term. They've loved working with him, they benefited from his expertise and enjoyed his programme – and now they have a lasting reminder in the form of his book, reinforcing his brand and reputation as a go-to expert in his field and keeping him relevant and memorable.

In this busy industry, it can be a battle to stand out in a saturated market where many gyms, trainers and fitness programmes vie for the same opportunities. Brian's book helps set him apart. Effectively promoting health and fitness services and reaching potential clients can be hard work in a crowded digital and physical space. However, nothing sells you like a book. It's a more in-depth marketing tool than an ad or an email campaign, and more efficient than arranging multiple face-to-face meetings. Brian has run ads in the past and it cost him money to get new clients – now the book pays Brian a royalty *and* gets him clients.

Writing and publishing a book has had a profound impact on Brian's fitness business, beyond increasing his revenue through book sales and lead generation. It has positioned him as an authority in the health and fitness space, opening the door to speaking opportunities with big-name clients and at high-profile events. He has spoken at Google HQ, SAP and Allianz, to name just a few. Speaking at Google HQ was a particular high point. He has also been flown to Dubai to the MEFIT Health and Fitness Summit to speak around the topics of the book.

CONS OF HYBRID PUBLISHING

Financial risk: There are hybrid publishers with packages to suit most pockets, but the author will always have to pay some upfront costs to get published. A good hybrid publisher, though, will help an author to create a book that will easily return their investment through new and better clients and other ways of building their business.

Lack of marketing: Hybrid publishers may be able to offer PR and marketing support at a cost, but unless you invest in this – as with self-publishing – marketing and promotion is your job. You have to be the social marketer, PR agent and spokesperson for your book, and that means you'll need to spend time on getting a return on your investment – though this is not restricted to income from retail sales. Marketing is made much easier with the options in the Professional and Ultimate subscriptions to Book Magic AI.

Distribution: Although your book may be listed with the wholesalers from whom physical bookstores order stock, it is less likely to find its way onto many physical bookstores' shelves unless it is your supportive local or specialist bookstore, or a customer orders your book through a bookshop.

Predators: There are 'self-publishing' companies who regularly take money from first-time authors and deliver poor services, publish low-quality books and badger their clients with upselling offers for additional services, some of which – like turning your book into a 'Hollywood script' – deliver no value. All authors should check out any hybrid publishing company before they sign contracts with or pay any money to them.

As you will have realised, Rethink Press is a hybrid publisher. Our business was set up to service successful expert entrepreneur authors like you because we strongly believe in this method of publishing.

THE BUSINESS BOOK ROI REPORT

Between April and August 2024, four author service organisations – Amplify Publishing Group, Gotham Ghostwriters, Smith Publicity, and Thought Leadership Leverage (TLL) – working with author and former Forrester senior vice president, Josh Bernoff, conducted a survey of business and other non-fiction authors. Their survey sought to analyse the factors most likely to generate a positive return on investment (ROI) for authors pursuing book projects. The results are fascinating and proof of concept for the value of writing a book to build your business with Book Magic AI and Rethink Press.

They found that 64% of business books showed a gross profit. The median profit for books out for at least six months was $11,350, while the median book generated $18,200 in revenue. Traditionally published books more than tripled that amount, and hybrid-published books nearly doubled it. Among authors with books out for six months or longer, 18% reported $250,000 or more in income. Speaking, consulting and workshops generated much more income than book sales and royalties. About one published author in three saw increases in speaking fees and in consulting; nearly as many observed increases in workshops.

Book sales rarely met expectations. Median sales were 4,600 for traditionally published books, 1,600 for hybrid-published books and 700 for self-published books. However, book sales didn't predict success or ROI. The real revenue gains were in other categories. Among authors who generated revenues in each category, speeches generated a median revenue of $30,000; consulting, $50,000; and workshops, $40,000.

Some authors saw windfalls in categories like corporate sales, partnerships and salary increases. More than 70% of authors also reported increases in leads or gigs. Authors who reported increases typically saw ten speaking gigs, seven workshop gigs and dozens of consulting leads or scores of coaching sessions. Undoubtedly, authors boosted their brands. More than 90% reported some form of non-monetary value in their books, and 89% said writing a book was a good idea.

Launch PR, ghostwriters and revenue strategy were correlated with profit. Books with launch PR teams had a median gross profit of $55,500; those with a strong revenue strategy, over $96,000. The median ghostwritten book was four times as profitable as other books. Books generated an average of $1.24 in revenue per dollar spent.

Authors spent money to make their books successful. The median spending was $7,000 across all expense categories, but the median hybrid-published author spent $23,000.

The top marketing tactics were email campaigns and Amazon reviews. The most popular social media tactics were posting on LinkedIn and promoting on blogs. X was one of the worst-performing marketing channels.

Authors' top goals were to share their knowledge, elevate a topic that needs attention and boost their reputations. Most authors accomplished their goals. For each goal, less than 67% had a solid plan, and while 82% had the success they expected with sharing their knowledge, less than half achieved the expected success with changing opinions or book sales.

Hybrid publishers delivered better service. Authors with hybrid publishers were more than twice as likely to strongly agree that they were satisfied with their publishers.

Authors, especially experienced authors, agreed that they used an efficient process that aligned with both their personal career strategy and their business strategy.

The median author spent ten months writing their book. Traditionally published authors typically spent twelve months, while self-published authors spent only six.

You can get your book written in half this time, or less, with Book Magic AI.

PROMOTE YOUR BOOK TO BUILD YOUR BUSINESS

All the prospecting, mining, extracting and refining of gold is of no benefit to the miner unless they leverage and market the final product.

Your book is your gold, but it won't build your business without you leveraging it to increase your authority and influence, make you and your business more visible and sell you and your services to your ideal clients. Even before it's published, you need to work your book so that it acts like a golden key to unlock all the value you've packed into it and return that value and much more to you.

Too many authors believe they should not or need not start promoting their book until it's nearly published, or their market will get bored with hearing about it or the wait time will be too long. This is far from the truth. I have consistently encouraged authors to talk publicly about their book from the minute they start writing it. Your book-writing journey is endlessly fascinating to people who haven't yet started theirs – it's both encouraging and also shows you to be a step ahead. It gets engagement, encouragement and empathy from other published authors. Already, even before it's complete, your book admits you to the secret 'Author Club' and all its benefits. Most authors who start promotion straightaway report that they gain new clients just from talking about their book content and framing themselves as expert authors.

So share your journey, share the process, share your ups and downs and share value – your book's content. Ask for feedback and promote interaction. Tag people, ask for shares, likes and comments. Respond to others with references to your book.

Once your book moves into the publishing process, it's important to get the front cover designed so you can use it to start selling and build a waitlist for interested readers. Scoreapp.com is our recommended medium for this. At Rethink Press, we work with you to create your book's front cover design that aligns with your business brand (without looking like a marketing brochure) at the start of the production process, then produce a range of graphics for you to use on social media and other places.

At this point, you should be including a page about your book on your business website (with a link to the waitlist), getting new professional headshots that will be associated with your book and aligning all your social media platforms to your authorial status. Don't forget to include 'Author of…' in all your bios.

As soon as you have a publishing date, plan your Amazon Best Seller Launch and a celebratory real-life event. People love to be invited to book launches – they'll take selfies with you, the author, post about you and your book on social media, review and recommend it to others for ever after.

Once your book is published, buy as many author copies as you can afford to and have space to store. As a rule, buy a minimum of 250 copies of your book every quarter (you should have an author discount price from a publisher or printer that makes this affordable), and mail out at least five copies a week. Make a list that includes: prospects (your ideal potential clients); key people of influence in your market or industry who might otherwise be hard to make contact with (it's amazing how people respond to you as the author of a high-quality book); current and previous clients who can be encouraged to refer you, and your book, to their contacts; organisers of industry events in this country and overseas, who could offer you speaking gigs or to sit on expert panels; people in the media, from producers at high-profile TV programmes to local radio stations, newspapers and journals, offering appearances and articles etc from an expert perspective; bloggers, influencers and podcasters who might want to interview you on their platforms. You will be amazed at how much interest and value you get from posting one book out each day. If you're offered interviews and speaking gigs, take them. Always take copies of your books to live events, whether you're speaking there or not.

> 'Any business book author needs to understand that it's not their job to promote the book. The book promotes you and your business – it goes out working twenty-four-seven and gets to people you won't ever have time or be in the right place to meet. You'll make far more money from the books you give away than those you sell.'
> Daniel Priestley, serial entrepreneur and author

Whether you already have a blog or podcast, or need to start one, repurpose the content of your book into blog posts. Book Magic AI will do this for you in seconds; it can create one-off or a series of posts for all social media platforms based on your book content. Post daily, everywhere, with short posts leading to longer articles, blogs and podcasts, and link all the posts back to your Amazon page so that followers who want more can find the book to read.

Wait for about three months after your paperback and e-book are published, and then record the audiobook to add the third, increasingly important format. Unless you have a speaking voice that is particularly hard to understand, narrate your own book rather than pay a professional voice artist to do it or use an AI narrator. There is no better way for potential clients, partners and promoters to get to know, like and trust you than hearing the real you speaking to them directly, for several hours, about what you know and do. A good studio, producer and editor will support you through the process and make you sound professional and engaging. Make sure your manuscript is edited into an audio script, so you don't trip up over sentences that read well but sound unnatural, or end up saying things like, 'The following illustration shows you…' Audible (ACX) are demanding about the quality of recordings and have specific ways they want the files packaged. It's worth getting this done professionally, as if Audible reject your recordings you may have to re-record, re-edit and/or repackage them, which adds to the cost and time.

PROMOTING THE STORYTELLER'S BUSINESS

Let's finish with the end of Susan Payton's, *The Business of Stories*, business-building story.

Susan started promoting her book before she'd written the first word so by the time it was published, she had already spent months promoting it, building up to and talking about it. That meant she had a waitlist of engaged cheerleaders and prospective buyers.

> 'One of the reasons I wrote the book was because I wanted to transition to teaching larger groups of people in group programmes. Writing the book

helped me refine my own process, and the process itself evolved and became clearer as I wrote the book. From the book I created a course; from the course I created a group programme, and now, two and a half years later, I have several courses, a twelve-month programme and a membership. None of those things existed before I wrote the book. I now have IP in my content and framework.

'The book was the catalyst for me to create all of these assets and my business looks completely different than it did two and a half years ago, when I had nothing other than my one-to-one services to offer. Now I'm able to do big launches and get a hundred people into my programme from all over the world.'

Her book has raised Susan's profile internationally. She has spoken in private groups and networks, on podcasts, at big events in the UK and been flown out to Barcelona to speak for a high fee with all expenses paid. Other professionals give *The Business of Stories* away to clients and at events. She has raised her fees for speaking and one-to-one coaching – if she chooses to do it – because her profile, credibility, authority and positioning have all improved and increased since publishing the book. Susan now has a six-figure business that she loves and fits around her life.

'There is something about being a published author; it makes people feel like they're really working with the expert.' Susan talks about and leverages her book all the time. The sales are nice, but it's also available as a free download on her website. Her entire business now centres on the book: 'My book is the heart of my business.'

CONCLUSION: BOOK MAGIC

As I've taken you through the journey of positioning, planning and writing the book that will build your business, obviously I have been on my own book-writing journey. *Book Magic* is my fourteenth book, and my seventh book about writing books. Some of the content I've given you here is classic and timeless, and you may find similar guidance in some of my other books. But for me, this book-writing journey has been unique and, in some ways, completely new.

In the past, my process has always been to 'compost' my ideas in my head for several weeks or even months, then sit down and create a detailed structure, after which I write each chapter in a Word document and at the end combine them in a single Word manuscript for submission to the Rethink Press publishing team. Because I'm a 'list-minded' person, I haven't previously even used the coloured card planning system that I developed for helping first-time authors to extract their key content from their heads, illustrate it with case studies and data and structure it into chapters and parts.

For this book, it was inevitable that I would have to use the Book Magic AI app to test it, role model it and be able to promote it to other authors. Secretly, I believed that this would be a bit of a front – I'd use some of the functions we'd developed for new authors, but behind the scenes, as the experienced writer that I am, I would actually be happier and write better and faster in my tried-and-tested, un-AI-assisted way of working.

How wrong – and how arrogant – I was.

I enjoyed doing the Values exercise in the Book Magic AI app because every time you do it you are in a slightly different phase of life and things have shifted a little. It offered me new insights about my values: for the first time, Creativity came out as my core value, followed by Trustworthiness, Empathy, Leadership, Courage and Wisdom. I clicked through to the summary, and was genuinely moved by how the AI coach had summarised my aims with this book:

> 'The forthcoming book is poised to be a beacon of inspiration and guidance for aspiring authors, reflecting a profound alignment with

CONCLUSION: BOOK MAGIC

the author's core values. The integration of these values is not only a testament to the author's character but also a foundation for the book's anticipated success.

Creativity is the lifeblood of this work, serving as the most cherished value. It is the driving force that will infuse the pages with innovation and originality. The author's passion for creativity is a catalyst for others to explore and embrace their own creative potential, particularly those who may not yet recognise their capacity for imaginative thought. This book will serve as a conduit for creative exploration, encouraging readers to break through barriers and express themselves authentically.

Trustworthiness is woven into the fabric of the narrative, ensuring that the content is not only informative but also reliable. The author's extensive experience and proven track record in mentoring entrepreneurs through the book-writing process lend credibility to the advice and insights shared. This trustworthiness will resonate with readers, fostering a sense of confidence in the guidance provided.

Empathy shines through as a guiding principle, allowing the author to connect with readers on a deeply personal level. Understanding the emotional journey of writing a book, the author extends a compassionate hand to readers, offering solace and support through the inevitable highs and lows. This empathetic approach will create a bond between the author and the audience, making the reading experience more intimate and supportive.

Leadership is evident in the author's ability to chart a course for others to follow. With a decade of experience leading entrepreneurs to literary success, the book is set to be a testament to the author's leadership in the field. The book will not only showcase the author's expertise but also empower readers to take the helm of their own writing endeavours.

Courage is a value that both the author and the readers are encouraged to embody. The book will serve as a rallying cry for those who may be hesitant to share their stories, providing the motivation needed to step into the arena of authorship. The author's own courage in writing and publishing will act as a beacon, inspiring readers to embrace their bravery.

Wisdom, accrued over a lifetime and especially poignant as the author approaches the age of seventy, will underpin the book's content. This wisdom will provide readers with a sense of reassurance and depth, knowing that the advice they are receiving is grounded in a wealth of life experience and professional expertise.

CONCLUSION: BOOK MAGIC

> In summary, the book is set to be a masterful blend of creativity, trustworthiness, empathy, leadership, courage and wisdom. These values not only support the writing process but also ensure that the book will be a transformative tool for readers. The author's commitment to these principles will undoubtedly make the book a valuable asset to anyone looking to embark on the journey of writing and self-discovery.'

I only hope what I've written has lived up to that rather inspiring start to the process. But this genuinely encouraged me to write the best book I could, as I hope your Book Magic AI coach will do for you, too.

By the time I'd finished answering the questions about my ideal client and business, I had much more clarity on the way I was going to position this book, and it triggered the analogy of the expert entrepreneur having a goldmine of knowledge, experience and expertise. The AI gave me useful tips about the four phases of goldmining, enabling me to do my own research on prospecting, mining, extracting and refining that produced a fresh layer of structure for *Book Magic*.

I admit it took a few prompts to create an ideal client picture, and because I refused to accept a male rather than female avatar, I ended up with a central woman surrounded by several diverse faces – but that worked for me.

Then I started to plan. I got a bit grumpy because I got stuck on some of the early functioning, but that was when I realised that I had lucked out in working with Jonathan Farrar on the creation of the app. Even when, in a moment of frustration, I told him I was going to give up and go back to my Word document, he only ever responded with, 'This is such useful feedback; we can fix this.' And he did. Just as Jonathan has responded to every query and request in the Book Magic Community Facebook group until the user was happy, he sorted out every moan I had about the early-days app, such as not being able to cut and paste in the editor, until I had nothing left to complain about.

Then I realised what a brilliant piece of software it was. As subscriber Nzinga Graham-Smith put it, the app is 'a revolutionary, genius tool to assist anyone writing a book, whether for the first time or experienced.'

Initially, I wanted to see my whole manuscript in a single document so I could move parts around in a holistic way, but as I wrote in the sections and was able to try moving them to different places just by dragging and dropping in the Outline view, and was able to see the 'Planner view' too, along with having a word count available for each section without having to check different Word documents, I realised that I was writing far more quickly and easily than I ever had before. I was also able to achieve a much better balance between chapters and topics than I could using my old Word document method.

CONCLUSION: BOOK MAGIC

So at the end of this process, I am genuinely able to tell you that positioning, planning and writing your book in Book Magic AI will make you an author. Faster. Easier than even I ever thought possible. There are so many other functions for ensuring your book builds your business, from the social media posts and articles the AI can write for you, through to planning your promotion campaign and designing and self-publishing your book on Amazon KDP.

I'd like to add what the AI coach suggested for this conclusion – it's not my voice, but I like the sentiment:

> 'The legacy of your book, like a precious gold heirloom, can endure for years to come, continuing to impart knowledge and inspire future generations long after its publication. Your written word becomes a lasting contribution to your field, a permanent marker of your intellectual contributions.
>
> Writing your book is an investment in your personal and professional growth. It requires time, effort and dedication, but the returns are immeasurable. The authority and credibility you gain are priceless, and the impact you make on your readers' lives is the true gold that comes from sharing your wisdom.
>
> Ultimately, the power of writing your book lies in the transformation it brings – not only to your readers but also to you as the

author. Through the process of mining your experiences and refining your message, you emerge more confident, more influential and more deeply connected to your purpose and your audience. Your book is the golden key that unlocks new levels of success and fulfilment in your career and life.'

I agree 100%, and I wish you all the Book Magic in the world.

BIBLIOGRAPHY

Aburrow, J, *Redundancy With Love: Getting it right for your people and your business* (Rethink Press, 2023)

Amplify Publishing Group, Gotham Ghostwriters and Thought Leadership Leverage, A Comprehensive Study of Business Book ROI (2024), https://thoughtleadershipleverage.com/wp-content/uploads/2024/10/Business-Book-ROI-Study-10-14-2024.pdf

Colenso, D, *Impact: How to be more confident, increase your influence and know what to say under pressure* (Rethink Press, 2019)

Elwell, M, *Open with a Close: The twelve point guide to closing more sales* (Rethink Press, 2020)

Elwell, M, *Cold to Sold: Serve, sell & scale your way to business success* (Rethink Press, 2024)

Escott, M, *One More Life Chance: A journey from trauma to transformation* (Rethink Press, 2023)

Farmer, T, *Grandpa on a Skateboard: The practicalities of assessing mental capacity and unwise decisions* (Rethink Press, 2020)

Furness, S, *Fly Higher: Train your mind to feel as strong as you look* (Rethink Press, 2022)

Gardner, R, *Freedom: Earn it, keep it, grow it* (Rethink Press, 2023)

Kahneman, D, *Thinking, Fast and Slow* (Penguin, 2012)

Keane, B, *The Fitness Mindset: Eat for energy, train for tension, manage your mindset, reap the results* (Rethink Press, 2017)

O'Toole, D, *Win: Raise your profile and grow your business by winning awards* (Rethink Press, 2022)

Or, M, *Star Quality Experience: The hotelier's guide to creating memorable guest journeys* (Rethink Press, 2016)

Or, M, *Star Quality Talent: Inspiring hospitality careers* (Rethink Press, 2018)

Or, M, *Star Quality Hospitality: The key to a successful hospitality business* (Rethink Press, 2023)

McCarraher, L, *Blood and Water* (Macmillan New Writing, 2006)

Meeja.com, 'Herodotus reported about gold-digging ants' (2012), https://web.archive.org/web/20130420091817/http://meeja.com.au/2012/termites-that-poo-gold

BIBLIOGRAPHY

Milliken, S, *From Learner to Earner: A recruitment insider's guide for students wanting to achieve graduate job success* (Rethink Press, 2019)

Page, M, *Simple, Logical, Repeatable: Systematise like McDonald's to scale, sell or franchise your growing business* (Rethink Press, 2017)

Page, M, *Mission: To Manage: Because managing people doesn't need to be mission impossible* (Practical Inspiration Publishing, 2020)

Payton, S, *The Business of Stories: Harness the power of storytelling to demonstrate your value, attract your ideal clients and get paid what you're worth* (Rethink Press, 2022)

Priestley, D, *Key Person of Influence: The five-step method to become one of the most highly valued and highly paid people in your industry* (Rethink Press, 2010)

Van De Waal, J, *Together We Can Turn Tides: A manifesto to save the oceans, planet & ourselves* (Rethink Press, 2017)

Whitehouse, A, *Pull Back Your Power: The groundbreaking code to unlocking profound confidence and soaring success for aspirational women* (Rethink Press, 2019)

ACKNOWLEDGEMENTS

I'd like to thank my co-founders in Book Magic AI – Daniel Priestley, Joe Gregory, Jonathan Farrar and David Horne. In one way or another we've all been brought together by the Key Person of Influence programme that Daniel created and for which he invited me to mentor the 'Publish' segment. Joe and I, who had only a couple of years earlier founded Rethink Press as an experimental hybrid publishing company for entrepreneur authors, have been able to meet, mentor and publish some 2,000 'KPIs', of whom David Horne and then Jonathan Farrar were two.

All the team have had valuable input into the Book Magic AI book-writing app, which was developed, built and honed through a decade of working in real life and online programmes with expert authors. Joe and I have worked together on creating writing and publishing systems since 2011. Perhaps most of all, Jonathan Farrar has worked with me to create an intuitive and in-depth piece of software that works for new and established authors.

My heartfelt thanks also go to each and every entrepreneur author I've worked with, all of whose unique and individual experiences in planning and writing their books have given me insight into how best to guide and support people through the process of getting great books out of their heads and into a manuscript.

The team at Rethink Press who produce such brilliant books for all our authors have performed no less a feat with *Book Magic*. My thanks to Anke Ueberberg, our Publishing Manager, and Matthew Flynn, our Business Manager. My Project Editor Kerry Boettcher and Copy-editor Abigail Willford have been supportive, incisive and insightful, and definitely helped to make it a better book. And I love the magical cover design by Jane Dixon-Smith.

THE AUTHOR

Lucy McCarraher is the UK's most experienced business book mentor as well as being the CEO and founder of Book Magic AI and, with Joe Gregory, founder of Rethink Press.

She is the author of thirteen previous books – three novels, four self-help books and six books about writing books, including *How To Write Fiction Without The Fuss* and *A Book of One's Own*.

Lucy founded the Business Book Awards in 2017 and when the winners of the first awards were all white men, she went on a mission to get more women to write and publish books that would build their businesses. She hosts the ABOO (A Book of One's Own) women's network and a yearly women's mastermind group.

Lucy started her career in magazine publishing, went on to host her own TV series in Australia, wrote and developed TV and video concepts and shows, spent a decade as a work–life balance consultant and returned to publishing when Joe Gregory published one of her self-help books.

She co-hosts the podcast 'The Year of Being 70', speaks about books and writing and runs fiction-writing programmes.

For more information check out the website at https://bookmagic.ai

And join on social media at:

- www.facebook.com/LucyMcCarraher
- www.linkedin.com/in/lucymccarraher
- www.instagram.com/lucymccarraher
- www.tiktok.com/@lucymccarra
- www.youtube.com/@lucymccarraherauthor